Emergence and Survival

# Contributions to Management Science

www.springer.com/series/1505

Oliver Falck

# Emergence and Survival of New Businesses

## Econometric Analyses

With 13 Figures and 31 Tables

Physica-Verlag

A Springer Company

Dr. Oliver Falck
Ifo Institute for Economic Research
Poschingerstr. 5
81679 München
Germany
falck@ifo.de

Library of Congress Control Number: 2007929535

ISSN 1431-1941
ISBN 978-3-7908-1947-2 Physica-Verlag Heidelberg New York

Physica-Verlag is a part of Springer Science+Business Media

springer.com

© Physica-Verlag Heidelberg 2007

Production: LE-TeX Jelonek, Schmidt & Vöckler GbR, Leipzig
Cover-design: WMX Design GmbH, Heidelberg

SPIN 12025022      42/3180YL - 5 4 3 2 1 0      Printed on acid-free paper

# Preface

The topic of new business formation and survival has generated extensive empirical research, covering numerous countries as well as varying time periods. However, there is still little evidence for business formation processes in Germany due to a lack of comprehensive data on new businesses. In this book, a unique dataset – provided by the Institute for Employment Research (IAB) - consisting of the population of all businesses with at least one employee under social security in Germany in all private industries is used to analyse the determinants of new business formation and survival in Germany. In doing this, this book contributes to the literature of international entrepreneurship research.

The chapters of this book are partially based on papers previously published. The permissions to reprint these papers granted by *Taylor & Francis* and by *Springer Science and Business Media* are gratefully acknowledged. The chapters can be read independently of each other.

Chapter 3 is based on joint work with Stephan Heblich, chapter 4 on joint work with Michael Fritsch, and chapter 5 on joint work with Udo Brixy and Michael Fritsch. I profited enormously from these fruitful cooperations.

Many people have provided further helpful comments. I especially thank John Addison, Lutz Bellmann, Gerhard Kleinhenz, as well as my colleagues and referees of the papers on which some chapters are based. The single chapters of this book were mainly written during my work at the Research Unit for Economic and Social Policy headed by Gerhard Kleinhenz at the University of Passau. I am grateful, that Gerhard Kleinhenz made this book possible by providing a generous print subsidy.

Furthermore, I want to thank Deborah Willow for providing careful editing and proofreading, and Angelika Wacker and Ingrid Grübl for their continuous support.

Finally, Barbara Fess and Gabriele Keidel at Springer have been tremendously helpful and encouraging in realising this book project.

*Oliver Falck*

# Contents

# 1 Introduction, Summary, and Conclusions

## 1.1 Basic Conditions in Germany: A Stylized Review

Germany's job market is in a deep crisis.[1] Economists are in general agreement that unemployment in Germany is not the result of economic cycles but is, instead, rooted in structural causes. The original German model of social market economy (*Soziale Marktwirtschaft*) emphasized the principle of subsidiarity and thus self-help. However, the development of unions and employer associations, and the resulting actions of political parties interested in the patronage of such entities, have changed the original German model into one of an all-embracing welfare state that guarantees individuals their acquired standard of living. This evolution is partly due to Germany's history of being a protected industrial society where labor agreements could be negotiated between employers and employees that promised noncompetitive wages regardless of the employees' productivity, a situation particularly true for unskilled and semi-skilled employees. Employers profited from conflict-free relations with their employees and thus from relatively few strike days. Individuals who remained unemployed due to non-market-clearing wages and excessive individual reservation wages did not suffer much, if at all, due to the elaborate welfare state that guaranteed them a high standard of living. In fact, there was very little incentive to seek full- or even part-time employment.

The world has changed dramatically in the last couple of decades, however. Globalization is on the steady increase due to improvement of transportation infrastructure and communication, increasing international capital mobility, and the collapse of the Eastern Bloc, as well as the reduction of trade barriers (e.g., the European Union). Enterprises are increasingly under pressure from international competition. Companies use their connections and networks to shift labor-intensive production to areas of the globe that can offer competitive wages, a situation that has had an espe-

---

[1] As the following analyses widely refer to West Germany (except for chapter 3), this short review will not focus on East-German-specific problems.

cially strong impact on low-skill jobs in the home country. In contrast, at least in Germany, capital-intensive production is not affected by shifting employment to low-cost countries. Rather than cheap labor, a highly developed infrastructure and a great degree of legal certainty are more important and beneficial to capital-intensive production. However, in the wake of the eastern enlargement of the European Union, even these factors will not be able to keep business in Germany as its neighbor states will also be able to guarantee these conditions.

Under these circumstances, it is no surprise that the promotion of business start-ups has been the focus of economic policy. The goal is to encourage employment-effective macroeconomic development. It is believed that innovative business start-ups, especially in the service sector, will create employment for those individuals whose jobs have been lost, particularly the secondary-sector employees. In addition to these direct job-creating effects, innovative business start-ups are expected to induce growth impulses (supply-side effects) due to the intensified competition they will engender, thus leading to efficiency gains and more innovation (cf. Fritsch and Mueller 2004; Fritsch et al. 2005).

It is the emergence and survival of these new businesses that is the subject of this introductory chapter, which proceeds as follows. Section 1.2 provides a short description of the data and the methods of analysis applied in this book. Section 1.3 summarizes the growth and employment effects of new business formation. Chapter 2 and 3 will treat these effects more extensively. Section 1.4 gives the main findings of chapters 4 through 6 on the determinants of the emergence and survival of new businesses. Section 1.5 summarizes the main theses of this book and draws some policy conclusions.

## 1.2 Data and Methods of Analysis

Direct, comprehensive data on new business formation are unavailable in Germany. However, it is possible to extract this sort of information from the German Social Insurance Statistics of the Federal Employment Services.[2] These statistics began to be collected in West Germany in 1973 and are derived from public health, pension, and unemployment insurance reports. Each business with at least one employee subject to social security receives a unique, permanently assigned code number; the code number is thus an identifier for the business. Thus, a code number occurring for the

---

[2] See Fritsch and Brixy (2004) for a description of this data source.

first time in the file signals the emergence of a start-up business. A disappearing number represents a closure. On the basis of these code numbers, the German Social Insurance Statistics can be reformulated as an *establishment file*, allowing analysis of business dynamics in the economy. The empirical data thus derived include two categories of new entities: new firm headquarters and new subsidiaries. For the purposes of this book, the term "new business" will be used to describe both types.

The information on new businesses and their survival drawn from the *establishment file* of the German Social Insurance Statistics can be complemented by data from a sample called the *establishment panel* provided by the Institute for Employment Research (IAB).[3] This data consists of the results of annual surveys of businesses that have been carried out in West Germany since 1993. The businesses are selected for survey according to the principle of optimum stratification of the random sample. The probability of a business being selected increases with its size. Thus, the *IAB establishment panel* contains relatively more larger-scale businesses compared to their proportion in the entire population of businesses with at least one employee subject to social security. The surveyed businesses are annually given a catalogue of questions concerning their characteristics, such as number of employees and their qualifications, revenue, and investments. This catalogue guarantees the panel character of the survey. Additional sets of questions on, for example, working-time flexibility, overtime, and working-time accounts are included in selected annual catalogues.

The analyses presented in this book widely deal only with West Germany[4] for two reasons: (1) reliable data for East Germany are available only for a much shorter timespan and (2) East German business formation is driven by transformation processes and other factors that are substantially different from the factors that drive business start-up in West Germany.

The data is structured as a time-series cross-section, or panel, which must be analyzed using advanced econometric methods that are capable of accounting for the heterogeneity between cross-sections and the dynamics over time. Many econometric methods have been developed for such a task, ranging from simple panel correction of the standard errors in standard estimation methods like ordinary least squares to survival time analysis to panel distributed lag models and sophisticated panel error correction models.[5]

---

[3] See Bellmann (1997) for a description of this data source.
[4] Except for chapter 3.
[5] For a nontechnical overview, see Beck (2001).

## 1.3 Growth and Employment Effects of New Business Formation

Based on the *establishment file* of the German Social Insurance Statistics, Fritsch and Weyh (2006) calculate that for the start-up cohorts between 1984 and 2002, a yearly average of 303,395 persons are employed by newly founded businesses when looking at all private sectors combined. That is, for the yearly average of 132,970 new businesses, 42,352 persons are employed by 14,515 new manufacturing businesses, and 213,493 are employed by 98,984 new service sector businesses.[6] This results in an average business size of 2.28 employees over all start-up cohorts if taking into account all private sectors. For manufacturing, the average business size is 2.92; in the service sector it is 2.16. However, these numbers draw a too-optimistic picture of the direct employment effects. Newly created businesses have a high risk of failure, for various reasons. Fritsch and Weyh (2006) point out the consequences of this *liability of newness* (cf. Aldrich and Auster, 1986) for employment development: in manufacturing, average employment increases to about 120% of initial employment subsequent to entry; in the service sector, however, average employment starts to decrease in the second year after start-up and drops below initial employment size by approximately the seventh year after entry.

In addition to the direct job-creating effects are important indirect effects of new firm formation, effects that frequently take a long time to manifest. Fritsch and Mueller (2004) enumerate four of these indirect effects (supply-side effects): securing efficiency, acceleration of structural change, amplified innovation, and greater variety of products. Based on the *establishment file* of the German Social Insurance Statistics, Fritsch and Mueller (2004) state that the indirect job-creating effects of start-ups seem to be more strongly pronounced than the direct effects. The maximum positive influence of start-up indirect effects on regional employment development is reached after approximately eight years. Fritsch and Mueller analyze the long-term relationship between regional employment growth and start-up rates by means of an Almon-type panel distributed lag model.

Chapter 2 sheds light on these supply-side effects of new business formation on the industry level. Using the *establishment file* of the German Social Insurance Statistics, chapter 2 analyzes the effects of efficiency-guaranteeing *hit and run competition* (cf. Baumol et al. 1982) and of high-quality – innovative – new business formation on industry growth by

---

[6] Note that all private sectors consist of manufacturing, services and other private sectors like agriculture or construction.

means of a state-of-the-art dynamic panel error correction model. The results suggest that only high-quality innovative start-ups that survive for a longer time period have a positive influence on industry growth.

In this light, new business formation may provide a missing link in theories of endogenous growth, in the tradition of Romer (1986), which emphasize the influence of research and development on economic growth. Among other activities, private businesses generate new knowledge through research and development. This knowledge may be exploited by them or by other businesses competing in the same industry (cf. Mueller 2006b). One reason that the producer of such knowledge might not exploit it could be that it, as an incumbent firm, does not want to take the risks associated with new products or processes. The established firm might focus, instead, on exploiting the profit possibilities of its already existing products (cf. Geroski 1995; Audretsch 1995). Another explanation for poor exploitation of new knowledge by its producer might be the difficulty related to necessary reorganization measures – especially in established (large) businesses (cf. Jovanovic 2001). Entrepreneurial activity, setting up a business, and commercializing unexploited knowledge are mechanisms by which knowledge spillovers occur (cf. Mueller 2006b). Founders of new firms might have worked for incumbent firms or the new venture might be a new branch of an existing firm. Audretsch (1995) points out that many radical innovations have been introduced by new businesses rather than by incumbents. A key assumption (cf. Acs et al. 2004) is that new business formation diminishes the *knowledge filter* between the creation and exploitation of knowledge and therefore offers a possible mechanism of knowledge spillovers in Romer-style growth models. These knowledge spillover mechanisms have so far been a *black box* in endogenous growth theory.

This is all very well, but it must be kept in mind that knowledge diffusion can take place only when there exists a sophisticated and well-working regional network, which, in turn, depends on social institutions and the overall business culture. Thus there are some remaining regional competitive advantages — even in the "Age of Globalization." Chapter 3 engages in a quest to discover what these new "locational" factors might be and how and why they are necessary in creating dynamics and regional growth. In doing so, chapter 3 tries to link agglomeration advantages of the new economic geography with competitive advantages of Porter's cluster theory. But chapter 3 also goes beyond these approaches and adds further regional growth factors such as creativity or diversity. Using the *establishment file* of the German Social Insurance Statistics chapter 3 tries to find empirical evidence for this picture of the impact of modern location factors on regional dynamics.

Recapitulating, to understand the "true" impact of new business formation on (regional) growth and employment development, it is not sufficient to measure success merely by looking at the initial employment gains generated by business start-up. As the maximum positive influence of new business formation on (regional) growth and employment development occurs only indirectly through supply-side effects years after emergence, long-term survival is a more appropriate indicator of success. The factors most important for the emergence and survival of new businesses are the subject of the next section.

## 1.4 Determinants of the Emergence and Survival of New Businesses

The purpose of this section is to analyze the determinants of the emergence and (long-term) survival of new businesses. The analyses are based on the *establishment file* of the German Social Insurance Statistics and are partially complemented by information drawn from the IAB *establishment panel*.

In chapter 4, an initial analysis of the determinants of new business formation is made. A multi-dimensional approach is applied to simultaneously analyze the effects of three groups of determinants on new firm formation: industry, location, and change over time. A zero-inflated negative binomial count data model with panel corrected standard errors is applied. The analysis indicates that the regional dimension plays a key role in new business formation; thus, empirical study may gain important insight by accounting for location. There are at least three results of particular interest.

First, the positive influence of small business presence on new business formation that has been found in many cross-regional analyses arguing that small businesses are *hothouses for nascent entrepreneurs* (cf. Wagner 2004) may, to a considerable extent, be related to the minimum efficient size of the industries located in the region.

Second, chapter 4 demonstrates a significant positive relationship between the entrepreneurial character of an industry in a certain location and the number of start-ups. This finding clearly indicates that the characteristics of the technological regime and, therefore, of innovation processes play an important role in the formation of new businesses. The significant link between innovation and new business formation is further supported by the positive impact that is found in chapter 4 for the level of invention in a region and the number of start-ups.

Third, the different characteristics of large economic sectors have a remarkable effect on new business formation. A higher propensity to start a business can be found in the service sector as start-ups in the service sector require less industry-specific knowledge. Due to the different requirements of industry-specific knowledge, persons experiencing short-term unemployment are more likely to start up a service-sector business than they are to engage in a manufacturing venture, if, that is, they start any sort of business. However, long-term unemployment remains insignificant for both sectors. Furthermore, the indicator of minimum efficient size has greater importance in the service sector, suggesting a stronger entry-deterring effect of size requirements than is the case in the manufacturing sector.

Chapter 5 advances this line of research by analyzing the survival of newly founded businesses. Chapter 5 analyzes the impact of industry, region, and time on new business survival rates by means of a multi-dimensional approach. Using ordinary least squares with panel corrected standard errors, a set of variables is identified that have an impact on the survival chances of new businesses. By accounting for the spatial dimension, chapter 5 shows that the regional economic environment is of considerable importance for the success of such businesses. The impact of regional conditions is particularly strong for the number of start-ups in a region, regional innovation activity, regional employment growth, and population density. Moreover, chapter 5 finds pronounced spatial autocorrelation, which also emphasizes the importance of location in terms of "neighborhood effects." The impact of each tested variable always becomes stronger when it is disaggregated by region as compared to including the variable without regional differentiation. These findings clearly suggest that empirical analyses of new-firm survival should take regional level into account.

Chapter 6 also analyzes the survival chances of newly founded businesses. Chapter 6 differs from chapter 5 in two ways. First, in chapter 5, the econometric analysis is at the meso-level – the development of a number of start-ups in a cohort is examined over time. In contrast, a micro-econometric survival time analysis is conducted in chapter 6 to account for the increasing micro founding within the macro-economic theory, focusing in particular on the development of a single start-up over time. Second, chapter 6 includes information derived from the IAB *establishment panel*.

More specifically, chapter 6 analyzes the effect of industry, regional, and firm-level characteristics on the postentry performance of newly founded businesses by means of an econometric survival time model. First preference is given to an accelerated failure time model assuming a log-logistic distribution. The choice of this model is driven not only by technical exigencies but also by economic intuition. Ever since Gort and Klepper

(1982) and Agarwal (1998), there has been strong empirical evidence that business dynamics are driven by product lifecycle effects. For example, Agarwal and Audretsch (2001) find that the relationship between business size and the likelihood of survival does not hold for all stages of the product lifecycle. Therefore, the commonly used proportional Cox hazard model with covariates shifting the baseline hazard function by the same proportion at any time is not appropriate for measuring business success over time. Chapter 6 identifies a set of variables at the industry and regional level that have an impact on the survival chances of new businesses, findings that are similar to the meso-level variables found to be important in chapter 5. The most striking result is that at the firm-level, only business size has a positive impact on survival time. For many firm characteristics, such as legal form, foreign property, being part of a multi-unit firm, being a spinoff, or receiving national subsidies, survival functions do not differ when controlling for business size. Hence, business size appears to be a general measure of access to resources (e.g., being a part of a multi-unit firm, being a spinoff, or receiving national subsidies).

## 1.5 Summary and Policy Conclusions

Using the *establishment file* of the German Social Insurance Statistics, complemented by information from the IAB *establishment panel*, these analyses provide insight into the importance of new business formation for (regional) development and about the determinants of the emergence and survival of new businesses. These findings can be summarized as follows.

1. Supply-side effects of new business formation are key drivers for (regional) growth and employment development. It is not *hit and run competition* but, rather, high-quality innovative start-ups that generate growth.
2. The outstanding characteristics of dynamic regions in the sense of employment growth and net entry are the simultaneous existence of entrepreneurial spirit, creativity, and dominant manufacturing industries that are small businesses and dynamic. In such regions, the business services available probably concentrate on providing those services most necessary for young and/or small businesses, for example, financial services. It is not the *independent* existence of these factors that makes a dynamic region, but that they all occur *simultaneously*.
3. Innovative start-ups may be an important knowledge spillover mechanism in dynamic regions so can be regarded as an important part of the regional innovation system.

4. Short-term unemployment plays a considerable role in service-sector start-ups because such businesses need less industry-specific knowledge than would the start-up of a manufacturing business.
5. At the industry level, lifecycle effects and technological size advantages are important for new business formation and survival.
6. At the business level, only business size seems to be a good predictor for survival chances in that business size appears to be a general measure of access to financial resources and knowledge.
7. As it has been found that the characteristics of a business have a subordinate role in new business survival, the micro-econometric analyses currently in vogue appear to be overvalued.

Therefore, a policy aimed at stimulating new business formation should take the following into consideration.

1. As it is not possible *ex ante* to pick the high-quality innovative new businesses, society should trust in the market-selection process to pick the winners. The quality of the market-selection process is of crucial importance for new business formation to have a positive impact on industry growth. Policy should concentrate on designing an institutional framework favorable to entrepreneurship.
2. Because, at the business level, access to resources determines business survival, the policy should concentrate on enhancing access to financial resources and knowledge, for example, by establishing a market for equity capital for emerging start-ups, entrepreneurial education, or promoting network structures and science parks.[7]
3. The strong impact of regional characteristics on new business formation suggests that the policy should take the regional dimension into account. Therefore, it would be appropriate to involve regional authorities in such a policy or, alternatively, to shift political responsibility for new business formation to the regional level.

---

[7] A "science park" is a cluster of knowledge-based businesses, where support and advice are supplied to assist the businesses' growth. In most instances, science parks are associated with a center of technology such as a university or research institute.

# 2 The Effects of New Business Formation on Industry Growth[1]

## 2.1 Introduction

Does new business formation cause economic growth? Much recent research, initiated by Fritsch and Mueller (2004), has been devoted to this question (for an overview of this literature, see Fritsch 2007). Most studies find that long-run (supply-side) effects of new business formation are more pronounced than the direct short-run effects. Fritsch and Mueller (2004) enumerate four categories of these supply-side effects: securing efficiency, acceleration of structural change, amplified innovation, and greater variety of products. All research on this topic to date has in common that it analyzes the short-run and long-run relationship between new business formation and economic development by means of distributed lag models.

This chapter has two goals. First, it aims to distinguish between the different types of long-run supply-side effects. Second, dynamic panel techniques, which have recently resulted in fruitful research into the dynamics of economic growth, are used to model short-run and long-run effects of new business formation.

The remainder of this chapter is organized as follows. Section 2.2 discusses in more detail the two supply-side effects of new business formation — *securing efficiency* and *amplified innovation*. This discussion leads to the formulation of hypotheses to be tested. Section 2.3 describes the data. The estimation procedure is discussed in section 2.4. An evolutionary interpretation of the model will receive particular attention in this section. In section 2.5, results of the dynamic panel techniques are presented. The findings lead to conclusions about the design of policies aimed at promot-

---

[1] A short version of this chapter is published in *Applied Economics Letters* (Taylor & Francis) with the title *Mayflies and Long-Distance Runners: The Effects of New Business Formation on Industry Growth*.

ing new businesses and some ideas for further research, all described in section 2.6.

## 2.2 Long-Run Effects of New Business Formation on Growth

There are two prominent explanations for the positive correlation between new business formation and economic development.

One explanation concerns contesting established market positions. In the contestable markets approach, the threat posed by the possibility of new firms entering the market is taken to be a key determinant of existing firms' behaviour (cf. Baumol et al. 1982). Incumbent firms have an incentive to innovate so as to make entry into their market more difficult. Aghion et al. (2004, 2005) present a model of technologically advanced entry. Each potential entrant arrives with leading-edge technology. If the incumbent is less technologically advanced, the entrant will replace the incumbent. If the incumbent is also employing leading-edge technology, it can use its reputation advantage and block entry. In short, an incumbent who is approaching the development of leading-edge technology has a strong incentive to innovate and to keep pace with technological progress as doing so can prevent entry of competitors. However, an incumbent whose technology is out of date — regardless of whether it innovates — will find it difficult to keep pace with technological progress and, presumably, will not be able to prevent entry of leading-edge competitors. Consequently, an incumbent who is very behind the times technology-wise is discouraged from innovation.

The other explanation for the positive correlation between new business formation and economic growth is *amplified innovation*. Theories of endogenous growth in the tradition of Romer (1986) emphasize the influence of research and development on economic growth. For example, research and development can generate new knowledge, which may then be exploited either by its developer or by another business that competes in the same industry (see Mueller 2006b). When the actual developer of the new knowledge does not exploit it, and there are many reasons why it might not wish to (e.g., too risky), the knowledge can still "spill over" and lead to economic growth. One of the most obvious ways this could happen is that the founder of a new business who previously worked for the incumbent business might commercialize the unexploited knowledge or, alternatively, the incumbent could set up a new branch (see Mueller 2006b). Regardless of how spillover occurs, a key assumption (see Acs et al. 2004) is that new business formation diminishes the *knowledge filter* between the creation and exploitation of knowledge.

Below, the two hypotheses — secured efficiency by hit-and-run competition and amplified innovation as new business formation diminishes the knowledge filter — are tested by means of dynamic panel techniques.

## 2.3 Data

The analysis is carried out at the industry level, which was chosen due to data availability. Fritsch (1996) emphasizes that not only the industry dimension, but also the regional dimension, is of importance in explaining the impact of business population turbulence on economic growth. However, reliable, disaggregated data on changes in gross domestic product (GDP) as an indicator of economic development are available only at the industry level. Certain other indicators, such as employment development, are available also for the regional level, but all these other indicators have deficiencies. For example, suppose new business formation leads to labor-saving effects in the industry. This would, in turn, lead to a negative impact of new business formation on employment development even though the new business formation created efficiency gains in the industry. Therefore, the more reliable industry-level data are used for analysis.

The information on the number of existing and new businesses in an industry is generated from the German Social Insurance Statistics (for a description of this data source, see Fritsch and Brixy 2004). The data are comprised of the yearly number of existing and new businesses in West Germany for 44 private industries (manufacturing, construction, and services) from 1984 to 2001. The data set covers only businesses with at least one employee other than the founder; it does not include new businesses that remained very small (i.e., without any employees).

For each cohort it is possible to track the new businesses over time, which allows both hypotheses to be tested: Does the threat of hit-and-run competition secure a higher degree of efficiency in the industry? *and* Does new business formation lead to increased innovation by diminishing the knowledge filter? To test these hypotheses, two definitions are necessary. The *short-run start-up rate* is the number of new businesses surviving for only one year per 1,000 businesses. This rate is used as a proxy for the relative importance of hit-and-run competition in the respective industry. The *long-run start-up rate* is the number of new businesses surviving for at least five years per 1,000 existing businesses. The number of existing businesses is used as a proxy for the stock of knowledge in the industry, from which new businesses may benefit via spillovers. Assuming that long–lived new businesses are innovative or at least of high-quality, the long-run start-up rate can be used as an indicator for the diminished knowledge filter by new business formation. The industry GDP, in 1991 prices, is taken from the German Federal Statistical Office.

As new businesses must be tracked for at least five years to calculate the long-run start-up rate, the final panel data set covers 44 private industries over the time period 1984–1996. Descriptive statistics for the variables are set out in Tables 2.1a and 2.1b.

**Table 2.1a.** Descriptive Statistics, 1984-1996

| Industry | GDP (in billions) | | Number of businesses (in 1,000s) | |
|---|---|---|---|---|
| | mean | std. dev. | mean | std. dev. |
| Chemicals | 68.34 | 5.65 | 2.65 | 0.04 |
| Mineral oil processing | 39.52 | 7.04 | 0.12 | 0.00 |
| Plastics | 22.23 | 3.29 | 5.49 | 0.26 |
| Rubber | 8.20 | 0.41 | 0.82 | 0.01 |
| Stone and clay | 19.49 | 1.51 | 9.58 | 0.36 |
| Ceramics | 2.74 | 0.35 | 0.94 | 0.02 |
| Glass | 6.01 | 0.62 | 0.88 | 0.04 |
| Iron and steel | 14.97 | 0.89 | 0.18 | 0.01 |
| Nonferrous metals | 6.52 | 1.25 | 0.26 | 0.02 |
| Foundries | 7.59 | 0.85 | 0.91 | 0.02 |
| Steel processing | 20.87 | 2.38 | 20.08 | 0.36 |
| Steel and light metal construction | 14.17 | 1.63 | 5.84 | 0.78 |
| Machinery, gears, drive units, other machine parts | 85.92 | 7.03 | 12.26 | 0.78 |
| Office machinery and computers | 10.93 | 2.86 | 1.16 | 0.12 |
| Motor vehicles | 85.15 | 8.41 | 31.04 | 0.78 |
| Shipbuilding | 2.37 | 0.25 | 0.41 | 0.02 |
| Aerospace | 6.23 | 1.24 | 0.16 | 0.03 |
| Electronics | 88.81 | 9.61 | 14.14 | 1.16 |
| Fine mechanics, watches, and gauges | 14.70 | 1.25 | 10.74 | 0.99 |
| Iron and metal goods | 26.96 | 2.74 | 7.44 | 0.24 |
| Jewelry, musical instruments, and toys | 4.90 | 0.33 | 3.50 | 0.12 |
| Wood (excluding furniture) | 3.63 | 0.54 | 3.24 | 0.20 |
| Furniture | 20.13 | 1.08 | 33.62 | 0.29 |
| Paper making | 6.43 | 0.47 | 0.17 | 0.01 |
| Paper and board processing | 9.11 | 1.15 | 1.98 | 0.02 |

**Table 2.1a.** continued

| Industry | GDP (in billions) | | Number of businesses (in 1,000s) | |
|---|---|---|---|---|
| | mean | std. dev. | mean | std. dev. |
| Printing | 17.61 | 1.15 | 11.48 | 0.55 |
| Textiles | 13.04 | 1.93 | 3.47 | 0.31 |
| Leather | 3.32 | 0.52 | 4.24 | 0.27 |
| Apparel | 9.44 | 1.05 | 7.11 | 1.16 |
| Food | 44.95 | 1.67 | 44.00 | 4.97 |
| Beverages | 14.12 | 0.79 | 2.36 | 0.18 |
| Construction | 77.88 | 3.03 | 63.27 | 5.19 |
| Installation | 53.38 | 3.65 | 81.98 | 2.43 |
| Wholesale trade | 112.81 | 12.33 | 109.91 | 4.68 |
| Resale trade | 101.56 | 14.63 | 218.46 | 8.59 |
| Traffic and freight | 6.05 | 0.59 | 2.65 | 0.22 |
| Postal services | 59.37 | 11.11 | 59.03 | 5.13 |
| Banking and credit | 95.63 | 13.05 | 17.05 | 0.42 |
| Insurance | 29.98 | 5.90 | 17.68 | 2.47 |
| Real estate and housing | 180.14 | 20.55 | 33.74 | 5.37 |
| Hotels, restaurants, etc. | 30.97 | 2.12 | 110.49 | 7.25 |
| Science, publishing, etc. | 43.34 | 4.47 | 29.24 | 3.68 |
| Healthcare | 59.72 | 11.91 | 107.50 | 11.23 |
| Other private services | 307.33 | 81.89 | 197.48 | 22.62 |

**Table 2.1b.** Descriptive Statistics, 1984-1996

| Industry | long-run start-up rate (per 1,000 businesses) | | short-run start-up rate (per 1,000 businesses) | |
|---|---|---|---|---|
| | mean | std. dev. | mean | std. dev. |
| Chemicals | 32.24 | 4.39 | 10.94 | 2.40 |
| Mineral oil processing | 26.03 | 15.23 | 7.92 | 7.35 |
| Plastics | 40.54 | 5.89 | 14.25 | 2.70 |
| Rubber | 30.25 | 6.47 | 8.72 | 3.13 |
| Stone and clay | 24.00 | 1.76 | 7.19 | 0.92 |
| Ceramics | 40.80 | 9.34 | 16.60 | 5.36 |
| Glass | 30.00 | 6.51 | 13.14 | 4.28 |
| Iron and steel | 34.05 | 15.96 | 9.19 | 8.30 |
| Nonferrous metals | 48.51 | 12.90 | 16.90 | 7.46 |
| Foundries | 26.61 | 7.36 | 8.83 | 2.32 |
| Steel processing | 34.38 | 2.63 | 11.32 | 1.11 |
| Steel and light metal construction | 51.92 | 5.21 | 25.00 | 2.18 |
| Machinery, gears, drive units, other machine parts | 42.09 | 4.73 | 11.42 | 1.13 |

**Table 2.1b.** continued

| Industry | long-run start-up rate (per 1,000 businesses) | | short-run start-up rate (per 1,000 businesses) | |
|---|---|---|---|---|
| | mean | std. dev. | mean | std. dev. |
| Office machinery and computers | 59.67 | 11.22 | 21.58 | 3.57 |
| Motor vehicles | 36.02 | 4.29 | 10.25 | 0.94 |
| Shipbuilding | 38.52 | 13.63 | 16.54 | 6.69 |
| Aerospace | 59.40 | 17.71 | 19.92 | 11.53 |
| Electronics | 47.66 | 5.42 | 14.60 | 1.29 |
| Fine mechanics, watches, and gauges | 49.27 | 4.99 | 7.89 | 1.35 |
| Iron and metal goods | 36.33 | 2.81 | 12.01 | 1.39 |
| Jewelry, musical instruments, and toys | 36.20 | 7.30 | 14.21 | 3.21 |
| Wood (excluding furniture) | 17.21 | 2.89 | 7.18 | 1.92 |
| Furniture | 32.15 | 2.32 | 11.21 | 1.38 |
| Paper making | 31.61 | 11.21 | 14.08 | 12.97 |
| Paper and board processing | 30.05 | 5.02 | 10.59 | 2.82 |
| Printing | 38.41 | 4.42 | 12.61 | 1.68 |
| Textiles | 24.79 | 4.49 | 12.56 | 1.68 |
| Leather | 28.67 | 3.20 | 14.64 | 2.55 |
| Apparel | 27.45 | 3.24 | 23.34 | 2.29 |
| Food | 19.53 | 1.18 | 6.16 | 0.58 |
| Beverages | 13.75 | 2.79 | 5.73 | 1.85 |
| Construction | 40.08 | 3.50 | 29.11 | 5.66 |
| Installation | 34.23 | 2.90 | 10.31 | 1.19 |
| Wholesale trade | 44.38 | 2.98 | 22.50 | 1.50 |
| Resale trade | 44.44 | 2.80 | 22.65 | 2.12 |
| Traffic and freight | 42.92 | 7.45 | 16.25 | 3.20 |
| Postal services | 50.06 | 2.69 | 28.69 | 2.09 |
| Banking and credit | 23.48 | 2.76 | 11.15 | 1.71 |
| Insurance | 57.50 | 10.95 | 31.23 | 7.38 |
| Real estate and housing | 56.61 | 3.18 | 36.47 | 4.52 |
| Hotels, restaurants, etc. | 52.64 | 3.15 | 49.43 | 3.95 |
| Science, publishing, etc. | 61.06 | 4.82 | 39.26 | 6.60 |
| Healthcare | 53.30 | 4.78 | 7.12 | 0.79 |
| Other private services | 52.15 | 2.48 | 20.84 | 1.20 |

A graphical inspection of the time series data (Figures 2.1, 2.2, and 2.3) reveals that some are trending over time. There are two types of time trends of importance. First, a deterministic trend in a time series can explain the time series in terms of time itself. The relationship may be

$Y_t = \alpha + \beta t + \upsilon_t$, where $\alpha$ is an unknown intercept, $\beta t$ the linear deterministic trend, and $\upsilon_t$ a random variable with mean of zero. The second type of trend, stochastic, is similar to a deterministic one, but instead of the trending variable changing by constant increments each period, it changes by a random amount. A stochastic trend is defined as $Y_t = Y_{t-1} + \alpha + \upsilon_t$ or $Y_t - Y_{t-1} = \alpha + \upsilon_t$, where, again, $\alpha$ is the intercept and $\upsilon_t$ a random variable with mean of zero. Hence, the time series' change over time is at random. The ordinary least squares estimator remains consistent and asymptotically normally distributed in models including variables with a deterministic trend. In contrast, in models that include stochastically trending disturbances, estimators that are usually consistent and asymptotically normally distributed lose those attributes, that is, the estimators are not consistent nor normally distributed.

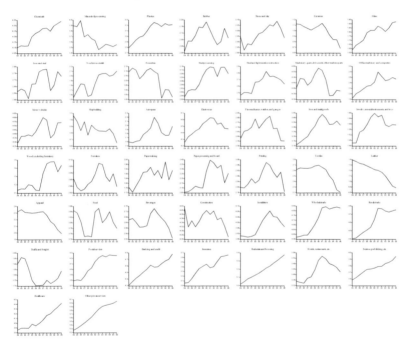

**Fig. 2.1.** Industry GDP (log), 1984–1996

To test for a stochastic trend in the time series data analyzed in this chapter, the general relationship $Y_{it} = \rho Y_{it-1} + \alpha_i + \beta_i t + \upsilon_{it}$ is applied, where $\alpha_i$ is an industry-specific intercept, $\beta_i t$ is an industry-specific deterministic trend, and $\upsilon_{it}$ is a random variable with mean of zero. An industry-specific intercept and deterministic trend are included only if the graphs of each time series suggest their existence. If a stochastic trend does not exist, $\rho$ is assumed to be zero; if a stochastic trend exists, $\rho$ is one. In the latter case, the time series is assumed to have a unit root or to be nonstationary. To test the nonstationarity of the variables, panel unit root tests are carried out by the method proposed by Im et al. (2002). Industry-specific intercepts are considered for all four variables — GDP (log), number of businesses (log), short-run start-up rate, and long-run start-up rate. The corresponding graphs suggest that for the industry GDP (log) and the number of businesses (log) variables a deterministic trend is added. Table 2.2 shows the results of the tests, which are straightforward: the GDP (log) and number of businesses (log) variables have a unit root, i.e., are nonstationary. After taking first differences of these variables they become stationary, i.e., they are both integrated of order one. In contrast, the short-run start-up rate and long-run start-up rate variables are stationary and, therefore, do not include a stochastic trend.

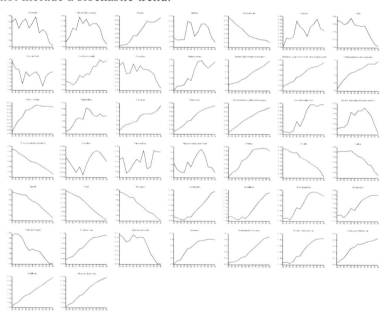

**Fig. 2.2.** Number of businesses (log) in industry, 1984–1996

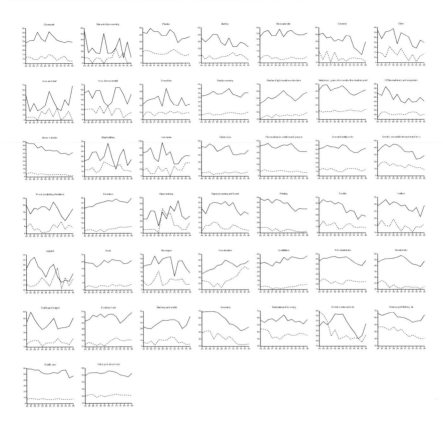

**Fig. 2.3.** Short-run start-up rate (dashed line) and long-run start-up rate (continuous line) in industry, 1984–1996

**Table 2.2.** Panel unit root test

| Variable | Test statistic | p value |
|---|---|---|
| Gross domestic product (log) | 2.04 | 0.98 |
| Δ Gross domestic product (log) | −8.07 | 0.00 |
| Number of businesses (log) | 5.10 | 1.00 |
| Δ Number of businesses (log) | −7.81 | 0.00 |
| Long-run start-up rate | −4.10 | 0.00 |
| Short-run start-up rate | −8.15 | 0.00 |

Number of cross-sections = 44. Number of time periods = 13. Individual effects (all variables) and time trends (gross domestic product (log) and number of businesses (log)). Null hypothesis: unit root (individual unit root process). Lagged differences are included according to the modified Schwarz-criterion.

## 2.4 Estimation Procedure

Determining the order of integration for the variables is important for setting up the analysis. If two or more variables are integrated of the same order, one may assume a long-run equilibrium between them. A linear combination of two or more nonstationary series that is stationary means that the nonstationary time series are cointegrated. Only the nonstationary series enter the cointegration relationship. Estimating this relationship by standard OLS leads to consistent estimators as the disturbances, i.e., the linear combinations, do not contain a stochastic trend. The disturbances are assumed to be stationary. All stationary variables enter as exogenous variables in the estimation of the corresponding (short-run) error correction model. The error correction model describes the short-run relationship of the cointegrated variables and how the variables adjust to the long-run relationship when they stray from it. In the error correction model, the exogeneous variables act as shocks that destabilize the long-run relationship.

The results of the unit root tests support a long-run relationship between the industry GDP (log) and the number of businesses (B) in the industry (log). The long-run relationship represents the underlying production condition in the industry:

$$\log(GDP)_{it} = \alpha_i + \beta \cdot \log(B)_{it} + \varepsilon_{it} \tag{2.1}$$

In Equation 2.1, the industry-specific intercept $\alpha_i$ stands for the long-run yearly direct and indirect contribution of a representative business to the GDP (log) in the industry under investigation. The slope coefficient $\beta$ is assumed to be one for all industries. It can be interpreted as a long-run elasticity: if the number of representative businesses in the industry grows by 1%, the industry GDP also increases by 1%. $\varepsilon_{it}$ represents an error term.

This finding of a long-run relationship between the industry GDP (log) and the number of businesses in the industry (log) is consistent with the findings of Agarwal (1998). Agarwal shows the evolution of industries through regularities in the time paths of key industry variables, in particular the number of firms (*Numfirm*) and the price and quantity of a product. In her analysis, the number of firms and the product of price × quantity also follow a common trend. Actually, Agarwal only models deterministic trends in the form:

$$Numfirm = \delta_1 + \delta_2 Age - \delta_3 Age^2 + v$$
$$\log(\Pr ice) = \beta_1 - \beta_2 Age + \beta_3 Age^2 + w$$
$$\log(Quantity) = \chi_1 + \chi_2 Age - \chi_3 Age^2 + z \tag{2.2}$$
$$\log(\Pr ice \cdot Quantity) = \alpha_1 + \alpha_2 Age - \alpha_3 Age^2 + u$$
$$\alpha_1 = \beta_1 + \chi_1, \alpha_2 = \chi_2 - \beta_2, \alpha_3 = \beta_3 - \chi_3, u = w + z$$

Nevertheless, Agarwal's research supports an evolutionary (i.e., an industry product lifecycle) interpretation of the long-run relationship between industry GDP and number of businesses in the industry as set out in this chapter.

The stationary variables now enter the short-run error correction model that is estimated in first differences:

$$\Delta\log(GDP)_{it} = \beta_{0i}t + \beta_1 \cdot \Delta\log(B)_{it} + \beta_2 \cdot SR_{it} + \beta_3 \cdot LR_{it} + \beta_4 \cdot ERT_{it-1} + \upsilon_{it} \tag{2.3}$$

To account for industry-specific business cycles, deterministic industry-specific time trends $\beta_{0i}t$ are included in the short-run model. In Equation 2.3, $\beta_1$ is now the short-run elasticity. According to the two hypotheses being explored, positive slope coefficients $\beta_2$ for the short-run start-up rate (SR; the hit-and-run hypothesis) and $\beta_3$ for the long-run start-up rate (LR; the amplified innovation hypothesis) are expected. The error correction term (ERT) is calculated from the estimated residuals of the long-run model. These residuals are the deviations from the long-run equilibrium. Consequently, $\beta_4$ must be negative and represents the average speed of adjustment to equilibrium across all industries. $\upsilon_{it}$ represents an error term.

## 2.5 Results

Table 2.3 shows the results of the long-run and short-run error correction models. As there might be a certain degree of multicollinearity between the short-run start-up rate and long-run start-up rate variables, the error correction model was carried out in different specifications, either including both variables or including only one of the two variables.

**Table 2.3.** Results

| Variable | Coefficient | t statistic |
|---|---|---|
| *Long-run model (dependent variable: gross domestic product (log))* *with industry-specific intercepts (not reported in this table)* | | |
| Number of businesses (log) | 0.9291*** | 4.10 |
| *Short-run Model I (dependent variable: $\Delta$ gross domestic product (log))* *with industry-specific time trends (not reported in this table)* | | |
| $\Delta$ Number of businesses (log) | 0.6311*** | 4.25 |
| Long-run start-up rate | 0.0003*** | 2.56 |
| Error correction term | −0.2541*** | −9.09 |
| *Short-run Model II (dependent variable: $\Delta$ gross domestic product (log))* *with industry-specific time trends (not reported in this table)* | | |
| $\Delta$ Number of businesses (log) | 0.7852*** | 5.40 |
| Short-run start-up rate | 0.0001 | 0.45 |
| Error correction term | −0.2708*** | −9.69 |
| *Short-run Model III (dependent variable: $\Delta$ gross domestic product (log))* *with industry-specific time trends (not reported in this table)* | | |
| $\Delta$ Number of businesses (log) | 0.6629*** | 4.46 |
| Long-run start-up rate | 0.0007*** | 3.25 |
| Short-run start-up rate | −0.0009** | −2.03 |
| Error correction term | −0.2584*** | −9.25 |

***: statistically significant at the 1 percent level. **: statistically significant at the 5 percent level. *: statistically significant at the 10 percent level.

Before interpreting the results, the estimated long-run relationship needs to be tested for cointegration. Cointegration analysis is carried out using seven tests proposed by Pedroni (1999). Table 2.4 shows the results of these seven test statistics. The cointegration tests result in a somewhat conflicting pattern. For panels with a small number of observations, the ADF-based statistics are most suitable and indicate the existence of cointegration and, therefore, the existence of a long-run relationship between industry GDP (log) and the number of businesses (log) in the industry.

The slope coefficient in the long-run equation is, as expected, significantly positive and close to one. The short-run elasticity between industry GDP and the number of businesses in the industry is much smaller than the long-run elasticity. This finding is in accordance with the findings of Fritsch and Mueller (2004), who emphasize the relative importance of the long-run effects. The coefficient of the error correction term is significantly negative in all short-run models, which signals a stable long-run equilibrium.

**Table 2.4.** Cointegration test for the long-run model

| Statistic | Test statistic | p value |
|---|---|---|
| Panel $v$ -stat | 2.89 | 0.99 |
| Panel $\rho$ -stat | −0.60 | 0.27 |
| Panel PP-stat | −1.81 | 0.04 |
| Panel ADF-stat | −3.32 | 0.00 |
| Group $\rho$ -stat | 2.53 | 0.99 |
| Group PP-stat | −0.11 | 0.45 |
| Group ADF-stat | −2.29 | 0.01 |

Number of cross-sections = 44. Number of time periods = 13.
All reported values are distributed N(0,1) under null of
unit root or no cointegration.

The results confirm the hypothesis of a diminished knowledge filter by long-run startups. The slope coefficient for the long-run start-up rate is significantly positive. However, the hit-and-run competition hypothesis has not been confirmed by empirical evidence. The slope coefficient for the short-run start-up rate is either significantly negative or not significantly different from zero.

The industry-specific intercepts in the long-run model are reported in Table 2.5. These intercepts permit discovery of the long-run annual direct and indirect contribution of a representative business to the GDP of the industry under investigation. The average contribution across all industries is 23.2 million German marks. However, as only those businesses with at least one employee covered by social security are considered whereas GDP is looked at for the industry as a whole, this value overestimates the impact of long-run successful businesses on industry GDP.

As the influence of the short-run start-up rate and the long-run start-up rate may vary at different stages of the industry lifecycle, in a second step, the slope coefficients are allowed to be different, depending on the phase of the industry lifecycle. Gort and Klepper's (1982) view of entry is that systematic changes occur in the sources of innovations over the product lifecycle. They argue that in the early phase of a product lifecycle, most innovations originate outside the set of current producers (e.g., from firms in technologically-related markets, independent inventors, etc.). Innovative entries should play a crucial role in this phase. In later phases of the product lifecycle, however, innovations are more likely to originate from a process of learning-by-doing. The cumulative stock of such innovations operates as an entry barrier and hinders entry.

**Table 2.5.** Industry-specific intercepts $\alpha_i$

| Industry | log(GDP) $\alpha_i$ | GDP (billions) |
|---|---|---|
| Chemicals | -3.10 | 0.0460 |
| Mineral oil processing | -0.75 | 0.4754 |
| Plastics | -4.91 | 0.0076 |
| Rubber | -4.13 | 0.0165 |
| Stone and clay | -5.55 | 0.0040 |
| Ceramics | -5.36 | 0.0049 |
| Glass | -4.51 | 0.0114 |
| Iron and steel | -2.09 | 0.1249 |
| Nonferrous metals | -3.32 | 0.0370 |
| Foundries | -4.31 | 0.0139 |
| Steel processing | -6.17 | 0.0022 |
| Steel and light metal construction | -5.41 | 0.0047 |
| Machinery, gears, drive units other machine parts | -4.30 | 0.0140 |
| Office machinery and computers | -4.19 | 0.0155 |
| Motor vehicles | -5.17 | 0.0059 |
| Shipbuilding | -4.73 | 0.0091 |
| Aerospace | -2.89 | 0.0568 |
| Electronics | -4.40 | 0.0127 |
| Fine mechanics, watches, and gauges | -5.94 | 0.0028 |
| Iron and metal goods | -4.99 | 0.0070 |
| Jewelry, musical instruments, and toys | -5.99 | 0.0026 |
| Wood (excluding furniture) | -6.23 | 0.0021 |
| Furniture | -6.68 | 0.0013 |
| Paper making | -2.90 | 0.0559 |
| Paper processing and board | -4.85 | 0.0081 |
| Printing | -5.82 | 0.0031 |
| Textiles | -5.01 | 0.0069 |
| Leather | -6.57 | 0.0015 |
| Apparel | -5.99 | 0.0026 |
| Food | -6.12 | 0.0023 |
| Beverages | -4.57 | 0.0107 |
| Construction | -5.91 | 0.0028 |
| Installation | -6.54 | 0.0015 |
| Wholesale trade | -6.06 | 0.0024 |
| Resale trade | -6.81 | 0.0012 |
| Traffic and freight | -5.53 | 0.0041 |
| Postal services | -6.14 | 0.0023 |
| Banking and credit | -4.50 | 0.0114 |
| Insurance | -5.70 | 0.0035 |
| Real estate and housing | -4.49 | 0.0116 |

**Table 2.5.** continued

| Industry | log(GDP) $\alpha_i$ | GDP (billions) |
|---|---|---|
| Hotels, restaurants, etc. | -7.36 | 0.0007 |
| Science, publishing, etc. | -5.78 | 0.0032 |
| Healthcare | -6.69 | 0.0013 |
| Other private services | -5.63 | 0.0037 |

Following Gort and Klepper (1982), the 44 industries studied in this chapter are classified into five lifecycle stages during the observation period 1984–1996.

- *Stage I* begins with the commercial introduction of new products and ends with a sharp increase in the rate of entry of new competitors.
- *Stage II* is the period of sharp increase in the number of producers.
- *Stage III* is the period during which the number of entrants is roughly balanced by the number of exiting firms.
- *Stage IV* is the period of negative net entry.
- *Stage V* is a second period of approximately zero net entry.

Industries were classified by visual inspection of the plotted series: there were 0 in Stage I, 23 in Stage II, 8 in Stage III, 11 in Stage IV, and 2 in Stage V. Table 2.6 shows the results of these modified models.

The results of the short-run error correction models are somewhat unexpected. Although the overall impacts of both the long-run and short-run start-up rates do not change much in comparison to the first reduced model (see Table 2.3), there are *no* differences between phases of the industry lifecycle. All interaction terms between start-up rate and dummies for the lifecycle phases are not significantly different from zero.

## 2.6 Discussion and Policy Conclusions

The results confirm the hypothesis of a diminished knowledge filter by long-run startups; however, no differences between phases of the industry lifecycle were found. In contrast, the hit-and-run competition hypothesis was not confirmed by empirical evidence. Potential competition already disciplines incumbent firms. Incumbents cannot exploit consumers by reducing output, raising prices, and earning supernormal profits in a market with small barriers to entry and exit. Consequently, short-run start-ups, having misinterpreted their market opportunities, are nothing but *mayflies* (Falck 2007a) — here today, gone tomorrow, making no mark upon the world, or, in terms more relevant to this paper, having no effect on economic growth.

**Table 2.6.** Results

| Variable | Coefficient | *t* statistic |
|---|---|---|
| *Long-run model (dependent variable: gross domestic product (log))* | | |
| *with industry-specific intercepts (not reported in this table)* | | |
| Number of businesses (log) | 0.9291*** | 4.10 |
| *Short-run Model I (dependent variable: Δ gross domestic product (log))* | | |
| *with industry-specific time trends (not reported in this table)* | | |
| Δ Number of businesses (log) | 0.6033*** | 3.99 |
| Long-run start-up rate | 0.0004*** | 2.48 |
| Long -run start-up rate * Stage III | 0.0001 | 0.30 |
| Long -run start-up rate * Stage IV | −0.0005 | −1.19 |
| Long -run start-up rate * Stage V | −0.0001 | −0.12 |
| Error correction term | −0.2602*** | −9.00 |
| *Short-run Model II (dependent variable: Δ gross domestic product (log))* | | |
| *with industry-specific time trends (not reported in this table)* | | |
| Δ Number of businesses (log) | 0.7794*** | 5.30 |
| Short-run start-up rate | 0.0001 | 0.32 |
| Short-run start-up rate * Stage III | 0.0001 | 0.20 |
| Short-run start-up rate * Stage IV | −0.0004 | −0.48 |
| Short-run start-up rate * Stage V | 0.0014 | 0.90 |
| Error correction term | −0.2719*** | −9.54 |
| *Short-run Model III (dependent variable: Δ gross domestic product (log))* | | |
| *with industry-specific time trends (not reported in this table)* | | |
| Δ Number of businesses (log) | 0.6231*** | 4.10 |
| Long-run start-up rate | 0.0009*** | 3.34 |
| Long -run start-up rate * Stage III | −0.0002 | −0.49 |
| Long -run start-up rate * Stage IV | −0.0008 | −0.87 |
| Long -run start-up rate * Stage V | −0.0011 | −1.15 |
| Short-run start-up rate | −0.0013** | −2.33 |
| Short-run start-up rate * Stage III | 0.0007 | 0.72 |
| Short-run start-up rate * Stage IV | 0.0008 | 0.41 |
| Short -run start-up rate * Stage V | 0.0032 | 1.52 |
| Error correction term | −0.2616*** | −9.06 |

Stage III, Stage IV, and Stage V are dummies with value of 1 if the industry is classified in the respective stage of the lifecycle.
***: statistically significant at the 1 percent level. **: statistically significant at the 5 percent level. *: statistically significant at the 10 percent level.

However, because long-run start-ups have a significantly positive impact on industry growth, economic policy should concern itself with these high-quality businesses, which could be called *long-distance runners*

(Falck 2007a) — they have the stamina and determination to stay the course. But, as it is not possible *ex ante* to distinguish the long-distance runners from the mayflies, society should trust in the market-selection process to pick the winners. The quality of the market-selection process is of crucial importance for new business formation to have a positive impact on industry growth. In this spirit, policy should concentrate on designing an institutional framework favorable to entrepreneurship. Storey (2003) identifies examples of such policy, including actions as diverse as entrepreneurial education, facilitating spin-offs from research institutions, reducing administrative burdens, and encouraging the emergence of a private market for seed or venture capital. One thing policy should *not* do is provide public funding for start-ups and thus disturb the market-selection process between publicly funded start-ups and other businesses that must succeed on their own.

# 3 New Businesses and Regional Development[1]

## 3.1 Introduction

Globalization has had an enormous impact on traditional industrial structures — one could even go so far as to say a "shattering" impact. Increasing competition has led to a greater variety of products at low price-cost
margins and sellers' markets are rapidly evolving into buyers' markets.
Today, consumers expect increasingly customized products so that mass
production capability is not necessarily the advantage it once was (Piore
and Sable 1984). This is especially true for the automotive industry
(Womack et al. 1990), where statistics show that producing two cars that
are exactly the same color and have exactly the same equipment options
happens about as often as a blue moon.

Customer demands for customized products and quick delivery necessi-
tate a highly flexible, fast-reacting production system. Increasing complex-
ity in production has led manufacturers to disaggregate the production
process by out-sourcing much of it, a strategy that originated in Japan and
is known as *lean production*.[2] In reducing vertical integration, manufacturers create an external supply chain, a process that has been made considerably easier by low transportation costs and an almost global communication infrastructure. Globalization has made it possible for manufacturers to
not only find, but to use, the cheapest inputs for their businesses. However,
it turns out that only the production of standardized and labor-intensive inputs has been shifted to countries with competitive labor costs; R&D and

---

[1] This chapter is based on Falck O, Heblich S (2007) Dynamic Clusters. *Bavarian
Program in Economics* BGPE Working Paper 16.

[2] "Lean production is 'lean' because it uses less of everything compared to mass
production—half the human effort in the factory, half the manufacturing space,
half the investment in tools, half the engineering hours to develop a new product
in half of the time. Also, it requires keeping far less than half the needed inven-
tory on side, results in many fewer defects, and produces a greater and ever
growing variety of products" (Womack et al. 1990, 13).

capital-intensive production tends to stay close to home. In the automobile industry, for example, it is generally true that first- and second-tier suppliers are located in direct proximity to the original equipment manufacturer (OEM). The low vertical integration in this industry necessitates close R&D coordination between OEM and important suppliers. This network is often complemented by universities and other research establishments, as well as by corresponding service providers. Taken together, this cooperative interlocking creates the sort of regional structure that Michael Porter (1990, 1998) calls a "cluster."[3]

In reality, some regions in a single industrialized country enjoy rapid economic growth while others are downsizing or stagnating. This leads to the conclusion that there must be some remaining regional competitive advantages — even in the "Age of Globalization". During the Industrial Revolution, the availability and accessibility of natural resources was critical to success and the basis for traditional agglomeration theories. For example, regional coal deposits attracted steel production, which led to surrounding and large industrial districts. However, today transportation costs have become less important and hence "traditional arguments for the existence of clusters have been undercut by the globalization of supply sources and markets" (Porter, 1998, p. 208). So, if some areas have a competitive advantage and it is not based on natural resource endowment, but still appears to be regional, what exactly is it? What are the "new" location factors conducive to innovation and growth?

The quest for postindustrial location factors is reflected in new economic theories that have as their goal understanding the comparative advantages of regions in an increasingly globalized environment. Seminal approaches include Porter's (1990, 1998) "theory of clusters", Krugman's (1991) "new economic geography", and Piore and Sable's (1984) "theory of collaborative economies". In general, all three approaches state that regions can compensate for potential disadvantages due to higher wages by setting up stable regional networks that literally bind companies to a certain region. This is good news, especially for those who see globalization as a job-destroying monster. However, when it comes to *how* this regional advantage can be achieved, the three approaches diverge. Porter highlights the importance of inter-industry clusters that will provide a competitive and supportive environment; Krugman focuses on the existence of large-scale firms with increasing returns to scale, leading to industry agglomera-

---

[3] "Clusters are geographic concentrations of interconnected companies; specialized suppliers; service providers; firms in related industries, and associated institutions (for example, universities, standard agencies, and trade associations) in particular fields that compete but also cooperate" (Porter 1998, 197f).

tion; Piore and Sable trust in the flexibility and social ties within industrial districts of small and medium sized specialized firms. All three approaches are looking at the same thing — drivers of regional growth — but from very different points of view, leading each of them to develop some similar, but many different, factors that might have an impact on regional development (Doeringer and Terkla 1995).

The quest for regional advantages resulting from the availability of modern location factors is our focus in section 3.2 of this chapter. We first look at how industrial agglomeration evolved up to the present day and come to the tentative conclusion that certain structures and factors support modern industrial agglomeration. Capturing the impact of modern location factors on regional dynamics though, that is, defining these factors and tracing them, is not an easy task as much of the relevant information is hidden between the lines of macroeconomic data. Jaffe et al. (1993) provide a clue in this quest for hidden information. They predict that there are traces of knowledge flows to be found in patent citations and they found evidence that these knowledge flows are geographically localized.[4] This finding inspired our attempt to trace modern location factors in Germany's dynamic regions. Section 3.3 introduces our data set and characterizes defined regions in Germany as either being dynamic or not. In this section, we begin to explore whether and to what extent the factors deduced previously are relevant to regional growth. The goal is to discover modern location factors that characterize dynamic regions, which are described in Section 3.4. Our conclusions and some political implications are found in Section 3.5.

## 3.2 "New" Location Factors

Traditional economic theory provides several location factors that support regional industrial agglomeration. Alfred Marshall (1890) introduced the concept of industrial districts to economic theory. He found that industries clustered around specific locations were taking advantage of external economies of scale. Marshall separated these economies of scale into three types: (1) economies resulting from access to a common labor market and shared public goods, such as infrastructure or educational institutions; (2) economies from saved transportation and transaction costs due to the regional proximity of firms along the supply chain; and (3) economies result-

---

[4] "[I]n principle, a citation of Patent X by Patent Y means that X represents a piece of previously existing knowledge upon which Y builds" (Jaffe et al. 1993).

ing from knowledge spillovers that result from "working on similar things and hence benefiting from each other's research" (Griliches 1992).

The existence of such location factors can attract more and more firms that are in the same industry as those already present, thus leading to an industrial agglomeration within a region. Some of the best-known examples of regional industrial agglomeration include the automobile manufacturing industry in southern Germany, the manufacturing belt in the northeastern United States, the footwear and fashion industry in northern Italy, or the former concentration of textile industry in Lancashire and Yorkshire in England, which was the subject of Alfred Marshall's analyses. Economies resulting from industry agglomeration within a region are also known as *localization economies* or *Marshall-Arrow-Romer externalities*. The Marshall-Arrow-Romer model predicts that local monopoly is more favorable to regional growth than local competition because intensive competition will reduce the appropriability of returns on investment and, therefore, also reduce incentive to invest (Feldman and Audretsch 1999). This argument reflects Marshall's influence and the circumstances of industrial production proceeded in his time. At the turn of the 20th century, industry structure was marked by mass production and economies of scale resulting from vertical integration and cost-saving process innovation. As transportation costs were high in those days, industrial agglomeration primarily occurred in areas endowed with mineral resources and in proximity to important suppliers, buyers, or consumers. Thus, industrial agglomeration was the result of *comparative cost advantages*.[5]

However, things have changed since Marshall's day, and so has the relative importance of his location factors. As economic wealth rose and markets became increasingly saturated with consumer goods, customers started demanding more individualized products, a process nicely illustrated by an example from the U.S. shirt production industry. Until the 1960s, men's shirts were a basic commodity and 70 percent of all shirts produced were white and of the same cut. By 1986, the market share of standardized white shirts decreased to 20 percent (Abernathy et al. 1999). Within a span of 20 years, uniformity was out; individuality in. This led to a change in production processes as individualized customer requirements could not be met with standardized mass production. Smaller batch numbers were produced and former economies of scale vanished. Manufacturers vertically disaggregated their production and started relying more on suppliers instead of producing everything themselves. Furthermore,

---

[5] Krugman (1991, 14ff) provides a simple model of geographic concentration based on the interaction of increasing returns, transportation costs, and demand that leads to comparative cost advantages.

economies from saved transportation costs are less important in today's world. Hence, Marshall's location factors need to be reexamined. The proximity of input-output relations pales in comparison with the rapidly rising importance of knowledge spillovers. What Acemoglu (2002) and Siegel (1999) describe as "skill biased technological change" has created an immense demand for skilled workers and hence knowledge in general. However, in contrast to other production factors, knowledge, in the form of human capital, sometimes also referred to as *tacit knowledge*, is comparatively immobile — even on the "information highway."[6] Tacit knowledge is a certain know-how learned by doing. It cannot be formalized or codified; rather, it is embodied in a person. Thus, von Hippel (1994) terms knowledge that is possessed by a person and, by extension, to a certain region, as *sticky knowledge*. It constantly circulates within a community's social network in the form of regular face-to-face communication and informal meetings. The close interconnection between the social and the economic network within a community (e.g., friends who work for different firms) makes knowledge spill over (Saxenian 1994) — it jumps, or runs, or "spills" from firm to firm via the social network. Thus, a community's social life acts as a knowledge multiplier, increasing the pool of geographically bound knowledge. This, in turn, fosters innovation and dynamics in the product lifecycle (Feldman 1994a, 1994b). In contrast to former comparative advantages deduced from a static cost-comparing point of view, competition and innovation now lead to dynamics and hence a *competitive advantage*.

Porter calls location factors such as raw material and unskilled labor "nonkey" factors or general use factors. Due to low-cost transportation and globalization, this type of factor is available everywhere today and thus can be obtained by every company. One might think of this factors as "inherited." In contrast, key factors, or specialized factors, in production are created. They include skilled labor, infrastructure, and capital. These manmade factors can lead to competitive advantage. Porter (1998, 208) combines the traditional theory of comparative advantages and dynamic theory of competition when he states: "To understand this role [of clusters in competition] requires embedding clusters in a broader and dynamic theory of competition that encompasses both cost and differentiation and both static efficiency and continuous improvement and innovation, and that recognizes a world of global factor and product markets." Thus, a cluster can influence competition in three ways: (1) it can improve the productivity of the firms within the cluster, thereby leading to process innovation;

---

[6] In contrast, information such as an exchange rate or a mathematical formula is codified and thus can be transferred.

(2) it can drive innovation within the cluster, thus fostering the product lifecycle; and (3) it can stimulate new businesses, which, again, foster the product lifecycle and might further promote new industry lifecycles. Competition results from an ongoing quest for future rents, to be derived from successful innovation-stimulating dynamics, and thus either invites the entry or forces the exit of firms. By introducing competition as a regional location factor, Porter is in accord with Jacobs's (1969) concept of *urbanization externalities* or *Jacobs externalities*. In contrast to the Marshall-Arrow-Romer model, this approach considers local competition, rather than local monopoly, to be a key regional growth factor.

Both approaches, the one by Marshall-Arrow-Romer as well as the one by Jacobs and Porter, are valuable in that they illuminate the concept of competition from different directions, namely, a static perspective and a dynamic perspective. The advantages of a local monopoly (static perspective; Marshall-Arrow-Romer) are covered in the literature on industrial organization. Competition is analyzed within the product market and hence at a certain stage of the product lifecycle. The focus of interest is the value chain. This perspective assumes that only intra-industry spillovers matter. In contrast, the local competition, or dynamic, perspective (Jacobs and Porter) attempts to explain the product lifecycle as being driven by competition for new ideas.[7] In this view, there is an emphasis on the importance of fresh ideas that result from inter-industry spillovers.[8] According to Gort and Klepper (1982), such inter-industry spillovers are most likely to occur in an early phase of the product lifecycle, they also find that most innovations originate outside the set of current producers, e.g., from entry of firms in technologically related markets or by way of independent inventors.

In line with Jacobs and Porter, Aghion and Howitt (2006) state that entry, exit, and firm turnover have an even greater effect than competition among incumbents on innovation and productivity growth, not only in the economy or region as a whole, but also within incumbent firms. There are two prominent explanations for the positive effect of entry on innovation and growth. One explanation concerns contesting established market positions. In the contestable markets approach, the threat posed by the possibility of new firms entering the market is taken to be a key determinant of existing firms' behavior (Baumol et al. 1982). Incumbent firms have an incentive to innovate so as to make entry into their market more difficult.

---

[7] Porter's (1990) diamond model for the competitive advantage of nations maps the relationships.

[8] For a more detailed discussion, see e.g., Audretsch and Feldman (2004) or Glaeser et al. (1992).

Aghion et al. (2004, 2005) present a model of technologically advanced entry. Each potential entrant arrives with leading-edge technology. If the incumbent is less technologically advanced, the entrant will replace the incumbent. If the incumbent is also employing leading-edge technology, it can use its reputation advantage and block entry. In short, an incumbent that is getting close to developing leading-edge technology has a strong incentive to continue its innovation and to keep pace with technological progress as doing so can prevent entry of competitors. However, an incumbent whose technology is out of date — regardless of whether it innovates — will find it difficult to keep pace with technological progress and, presumably, will not be able to prevent entry of leading-edge competitors. Consequently, an incumbent who is very behind the times technology-wise is discouraged from innovation.

The other explanation for the positive effect of entry on growth is amplified innovation by new firms. For example, research and development can generate new knowledge, which may then be exploited either by its developer or by another firm. When the actual developer of the new knowledge does not exploit it, and there are many reasons why he or she might not wish to do so, the knowledge can still 'spill over' and lead to economic growth. This is especially the case when the developer of new knowledge does not want to take the risk involved in with new products or processes. One of the most obvious ways knowledge spill-over can happen is when a person who previously worked for the incumbent firm becomes the founder of a new firm that commercializes the unexploited knowledge. Acs et al. (2004) present a growth model considering new firm formation that diminishes the *knowledge filter* between the creation and exploitation of knowledge.

According to Florida (2002b), it is not just the developer's pure knowledge that leads to innovation and it is not just competition that determines a region's potential for innovation and growth, it is the combination of these two factors with *creativity*. Thus creativity has a twofold impact on regional development. First, Florida defines human creativity as the ultimate economic resource. In doing so, he eventually presents a more precise categorization of the important input factor knowledge. While knowledge in general allows for production at a technologically high standard, successful R&D leading to ground-breaking inventions and thus future rents requires an exceptional kind of knowledge, namely, creativity. For example, if Thomas Edison had confined himself to simply making a more efficient candle, he would never have discovered the electric light bulb. Creativity is the ability to think "out of the box" and thus arrive at new ideas and better ways of doing things.

Second, Florida (2002a) and Glaeser et al. (2001) believe that a creative environment, including a rich cultural life and an overall bohemian lifestyle, is essential for attracting human capital and high-technology industries. They assume that bohemians contribute to a city's amenity and thus establish an environment that attracts talented and highly qualified individuals. This theory complements traditional agglomeration arguments: the prospect of a pool of high skilled workers favors the agglomeration of R&D-intensive companies, which, in turn, contributes to regional innovation and growth. Thus the presence of bohemians as a sort of magnet for creativity might also be a location factor contributing to regional growth.

## 3.3 Regional Growth Regimes

Our data are generated from the German Social Insurance Statistics (see Fritsch and Brixy, 2004, for a description of this data source). The Social Insurance Statistics requires every employer to report information about every employee subject to obligatory social insurance. The information collected can be transformed into an establishment file that provides longitudinal information about the establishments and their employees. As each establishment with at least one employee subject to social security has a permanent individual code number, start-ups and closures can be identified: the appearance of a new code number can be interpreted as a start-up, the disappearance of a code number can be interpreted as closure. Because the data are collected for the population of establishments that have at least one employee other than the founder, businesses having no employees are not included. The unit of measurement is the "establishment," not the company. The empirical data thus derived include two categories of entities: firm headquarters and subsidiaries. For the purposes of this analysis, the term "business" will be used to describe both types of entity.

Our information is available for Western Germany from 1987 to 2000 and for Eastern Germany from 1991 to 2000. This timespan is broken down into two periods. *Period I* starts in 1987 for West Germany and in 1991 for East Germany and ends in 1994. *Period II* starts in 1995 and ends in 2000. We have information differentiated by 52 private-sector industries (manufacturing, services, agriculture, and construction) and 97 planning regions. Planning regions are functional spatial units consisting of at least one city and the surrounding area (BBR, 2003).

**Table 3.1.** Descriptive statistics, mean values

| | | Western Germany | | Eastern Germany | |
|---|---|---|---|---|---|
| | | I | II | I | II |
| Performance | Employment Growth (%) | 1.98 | -0.13 | 1.55 | -1.70 |
| | Net Entry (‰) | 12.33 | 7.4 | 104.59 | 16.45 |
| Labor Market | Share of Highly Qualified Employees (%) | 3.36 | 4.49 | 1.91 | 6.02 |
| | Share of Engineers (%) | 1.95 | 2.29 | 0.98 | 2.45 |
| | Share of Small Business Employment (%) | 31.03 | 32.63 | 31.60 | 38.87 |
| Creative Class | Share of Bohemians (%) | 0.99 | 1.13 | 1.15 | 1.24 |
| | Share of Patents of Natural Persons (%) | --- | 26.62 | --- | 36.98 |
| Infrastructure | Type of Region | 3.51 | 3.51 | 4.14 | 4.14 |
| | Share of Patents of Universities (%) | --- | 2.5 | --- | 12.04 |
| Services | Share of Employment in Business Services (%) | 51.22 | 77.55 | 47.08 | 76.24 |
| | Share of Highly Qualified Employment in Business Services (%) | 7.62 | 9.51 | 3.86 | 10.68 |
| Inventions | Patent Density (‰) | --- | 74.5 | --- | 19.93 |
| Dominant Industries (Three Largest Manufacturing Industries) | Share of Employment (%) | 19.42 | 16.76 | 9.71 | 9.08 |
| | Share of Employment in Large Businesses (%) | 52.21 | 46.5 | 26.55 | 13.7 |
| | Share of Engineers in Large Businesses (%) | 73.37 | 66.3 | 35.23 | 28.42 |
| | Share of Small Business Employment (%) | 10.94 | 12.71 | 23.11 | 28.81 |
| | Net Entry (‰) | -1.32 | -11.96 | 27.00 | -12.66 |

**Table 3.2a.** Descriptive statistics, deviations from the mean values

|  |  | Entrepreneurial | | Routinized | |
|---|---|---|---|---|---|
|  |  | I | II | I | II |
| Performance | Employment Growth (%) | 1.45 | 0.64 | 0.55 | 0.29 |
|  | Net Entry (‰) | 6.17 | 3.09 | -5.00 | -2.73 |
| Labor Market | Share of Highly Qualified Employees (%) | -0.02 | -0.25 | -1.22 | 0.23 |
|  | Share of Engineers (%) | -0.19 | -0.15 | -0.6 | -0.02 |
|  | Share of Small Business Employment (%) | 1.07 | 0.93 | 2.98 | 1.78 |
| Creative Class | Share of Bohemians (%) | 0.06 | 0.02 | -0.15 | -0.07 |
|  | Share of Patents of Natural Persons (%) | --- | 1.57 | --- | 3.75 |
| Infrastructure | Type of Region | -0.13 | 0.07 | 0.95 | 0.62 |
|  | Share of Patents of Universities (%) | --- | -0.22 | --- | 0.07 |
| Services | Share of Employment in Business Services (%) | 3.29 | 1.77 | -4.04 | -1.69 |
|  | Share of Highly Qualified Employment in Business Services (%) | 0.35 | -0.22 | -2.34 | 0.50 |
| Inventions | Patent Density (‰) | --- | 1.33 | --- | 5.19 |
| Dominant Industries (Three Largest Manufacturing Industries) | Share of Employment (%) | -1.92 | 0.04 | -1.07 | -0.86 |
|  | Share of Employment in Large Businesses (%) | -5.59 | -0.32 | -9.48 | -3.87 |
|  | Share of Engineers in Large Businesses (%) | 3.05 | -0.17 | -12.70 | -5.91 |
|  | Share of Small Business Employment (%) | 1.71 | 0.80 | 2.94 | 2.92 |
|  | Net Entry (‰) | 4.52 | 5.14 | -3.28 | -0.49 |

**Table 3.2b.** Descriptive statistics, deviations from the mean values

| | | Revolving-door | | Downsizing | |
|---|---|---|---|---|---|
| | | I | II | I | II |
| Performance | Employment Growth (%) | -0.99 | -0.51 | -0.72 | -0.75 |
| | Net Entry (‰) | 3.52 | 1.63 | -4.63 | -3.48 |
| Labor Market | Share of Highly Qualified Employees (%) | 1.41 | 0.60 | -0.38 | -0.15 |
| | Share of Engineers (%) | 0.76 | 0.33 | -0.10 | 0.03 |
| | Share of Small Business Employment (%) | -4.48 | -1.78 | 1.16 | -1.35 |
| Creative Class | Share of Bohemians (%) | 0.14 | 0.07 | -0.06 | -0.03 |
| | Share of Patents of Natural Persons (%) | --- | -2.47 | --- | -3.06 |
| Infrastructure | Type of Region | -1.07 | -0.46 | 0.39 | -0.22 |
| | Share of Patents of Universities (%) | -- | -0.23 | --- | 0.39 |
| Services | Share of Employment in Business Services (%) | 5.32 | 4.26 | -4.92 | -3.89 |
| | Share of Highly Qualified Employment in Business Services (%) | 2.59 | 0.37 | -0.95 | -0.23 |
| Inventions | Patent Density (‰) | --- | -3.23 | --- | -3.18 |
| Dominant Industries (Three Largest Manufacturing Industries) | Share of Employment (%) | 1.06 | -0.63 | 1.53 | 0.86 |
| | Share of Employment in Large Businesses (%) | 11.66 | 6.62 | 1.05 | -1.06 |
| | Share of Engineers in Large Businesses (%) | 7.46 | 6.04 | 0.94 | 0.38 |
| | Share of Small Business Employment (%) | -4.63 | -2.28 | 0.79 | -1.59 |
| | Net Entry (‰) | 5.13 | 1.33 | -6.51 | -7.53 |

To measure the dynamics of the planning regions, we use the definition of regional growth regimes introduced by Audretsch and Fritsch (2002) and revisited by Fritsch and Mueller (2006). Under this system, regions with above-average growth rates and above-average start-up rates are

called "entrepreneurial." Regions with above-average growth rates but below-average start-up rates are "routinized." Regions with below-average
growth rates and above-average start-up rates are "revolving-doors," while
regions with below-average growth rates and below-average start-up rates
are "downsizing." These regimes can also be linked to the "old lifecycle
story" (see the seminal paper of Gort and Klepper 1982, for a knowledge
based interpretation of the lifecycle). Gort and Klepper's believe that systematic changes occur in the sources of innovations over the product lifecycle. They argue that in the early and adolescent phase of a product lifecycle, most innovations originate outside the set of current producers (e.g.,
from firms in technologically related markets, by way of independent inventors, etc.). Innovative entries should play a crucial role in this phase
(*entrepreneurial regimes*). In later and more mature phases of the product
lifecycle, however, innovations are more likely to originate from a process
of learning-by-doing. The cumulative stock of such innovations operates
as an entry barrier and hinders entry (*routinized regimes*). Among other
things, ongoing process innovations lead to outsourcing activities, resulting in new business opportunities. These new suppliers are non-innovative,
using nearly the same technology as the incumbents (*revolving-door regimes*). Incumbents that are not able to imitate permanent process innovations are forced to exit the market, resulting in a concentration process
(*downsizing regimes*).

**Table 3.3.** Number of different types of growth regimes

|  | Number of planning regions | |
| --- | --- | --- |
|  | **I** | **II** |
| Entrepreneurial | 22 | 37 |
| Routinized | 23 | 17 |
| Revolving-door | 27 | 16 |
| Downsizing | 25 | 27 |
| Upgrading | 34 | |
| Downgrading | 24 | |
| Unchanged entrepreneurial | 15 | |
| Unchanged routinized | 6 | |
| Unchanged revolving-door | 8 | |
| Unchanged downsizing | 10 | |

Employment and growth rates are closely related. In line with Gort and
Klepper, start-up rates are measured as net entry over the number of existing businesses. We expand upon the approaches of Audretsch and Fritsch
(2002) and Fritsch and Mueller (2006), who apply gross entry instead of

net entry.[9] Therefore, we have more information (closure) on which to base our classification. To account for business cycles and for structural differences between West and East Germany, averages are calculated separately for *Periods I* and *II* and for West and East Germany. Table 3.1 illustrates that the means of employment growth and net entry between East and West Germany differ. In particular, the extraordinary high net entry rate in East Germany is the result of that area's move toward a market economy. *Period I* is characterized by a growing economy; however, in *Period II* the economy declines. This results in positive employment growth rates and high net entry rates in *Period I* and negative employment growth and low but positive net entry rates in *Period II* in West and East Germany, respectively (see Table 3.1). Figure 3.1 shows the spatial distribution of the four types of region for *Period I*; Figure 3.2 does the same for *Period II*. Table 3.3 reports the number of planning regions categorized as entrepreneurial, routinized, revolving-door, or downsizing in *Periods I* and *II*. Proceeding from *Period I* to *Period II*, 15 planning regions are *unchanged entrepreneurial*, six are *unchanged routinized*, eight are *unchanged revolving-door*, and 10 are *unchanged downsizing*. 34 planning regions succeed to initiate new lifecycles and become more adolescent. For example, more than 25 percent of the planning regions classified as upgrading were revolving-door growth regimes in *Period I* but were entrepreneurial in *Period II*. This same pattern was frequently found by Fritsch and Mueller (2006). Further 24 planning regions mature along the lifecycle. For a spatial distribution of the dynamics of growth regimes see Figure 3.3.

To further characterize the planning regions, we define six groups of locations factors that have been found (cf. section 3.2) to be important for regional development. Table 3.1 summarizes the mean values and Tables 3.2a and 3.2b the deviations from the mean values by growth regimes of all variables described below.

The availability of a differentiated *labor market* in a region is measured by the number of highly qualified employees, engineers, and natural scientists and by the amount of small business (< 20 employees) employment in a region. Working in a small business may stimulate an entrepreneurial attitude and, therefore, increase the likelihood that the business's employees will consider starting their own businesses.

Whether or not the region is home to a *creative class* is measured as the share of bohemians subject to social security within the universe of all employees in the region and by the number of patents applied for by natural persons, under the assumption that these independent inventors can be

---

[9] They further apply the *labor market* approach instead of the *ecological approach* to calculate entry rates (for a discussion, see Audretsch and Fritsch 1994).

considered as highly creative. Our information on the regional distribution of patents is from the German Patent Atlas (Greif and Schmiedl, 2002) and is available only for *Period II* (1995 to 2000).

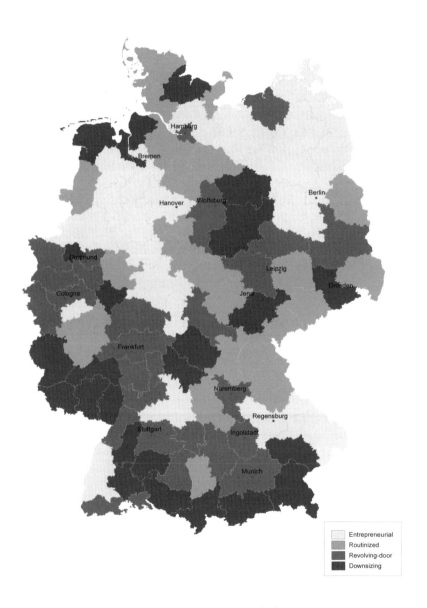

**Fig. 3.1.** Spatial distribution of growth regimes, Period I

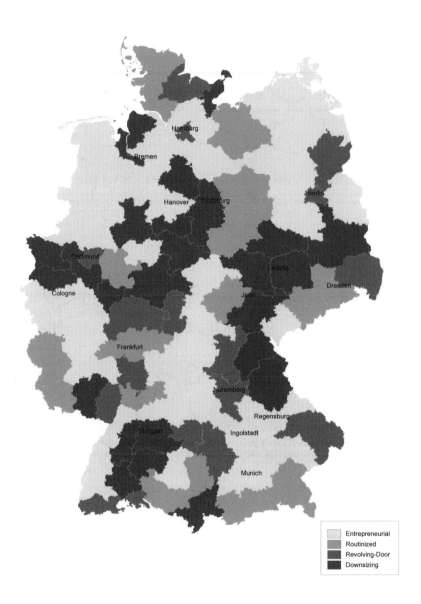

**Fig. 3.2.** Spatial distribution of growth regimes, Period II

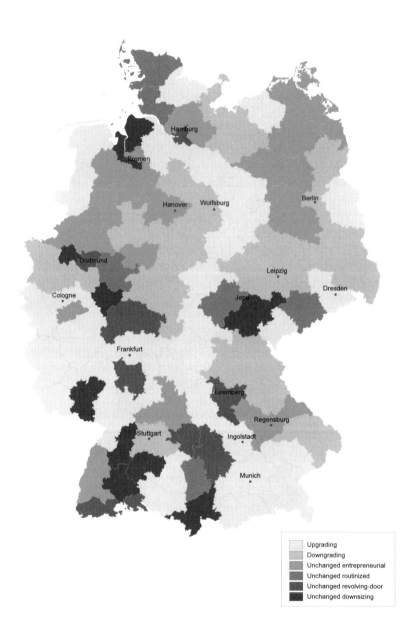

**Fig. 3.3.** Spatial distribution of the dynamics of growth regimes

**Table 3.4a.** Distribution of the larges manufacturing industries

| | Share (%) of planning regions where ... is one of the three largest manufacturing industries | | |
|---|---|---|---|
| | Upgrading | Downgrading | Unchanged entrepreneurial |
| Chemicals | 23.5 | 20.8 | 13.3 |
| Mineral oil processing | 0.0 | 4.2 | 0.0 |
| Plastics | 2.9 | 4.2 | 6.7 |
| Rubber | 0.0 | 0.0 | 0.0 |
| Stone and clay | 0.0 | 0.0 | 0.0 |
| Ceramics | 0.0 | 4.2 | 0.0 |
| Glass | 2.9 | 0.0 | 0.0 |
| Iron and steel | 5.9 | 4.2 | 0.0 |
| Nonferrous metals | 0.0 | 0.0 | 0.0 |
| Foundries | 0.0 | 0.0 | 0.0 |
| Steel processing | 2.9 | 8.3 | 0.0 |
| Metal construction | 5.9 | 20.8 | 0.0 |
| Machinery | 17.6 | 16.7 | 40.0 |
| Office machinery and computers | 11.8 | 0.0 | 6.7 |
| Motor vehicles | 79.4 | 50.0 | 73.3 |
| Shipbuilding | 2.9 | 0.0 | 6.7 |
| Aerospace | 2.9 | 0.0 | 0.0 |
| Electronics | 58.8 | 58.3 | 53.3 |
| Fine mechanics, watches, gauges | 0.0 | 8.3 | 0.0 |
| Iron and metal goods | 2.9 | 4.2 | 0.0 |
| Jewelry, musical instruments, and toys | 0.0 | 0.0 | 0.0 |
| Wood (excluding furniture) | 0.0 | 0.0 | 0.0 |
| Furniture | 17.6 | 12.5 | 33.3 |
| Paper making | 0.0 | 0.0 | 0.0 |
| Paper processing and board | 0.0 | 0.0 | 0.0 |
| Printing | 0.0 | 0.0 | 0.0 |
| Textiles | 0.0 | 8.3 | 0.0 |
| Leather | 0.0 | 0.0 | 0.0 |
| Apparel | 2.9 | 0.0 | 0.0 |
| Food | 58.8 | 75.0 | 66.7 |
| Beverages | 0.0 | 0.0 | 0.0 |

**Table 3.4b.** Distribution of the larges manufacturing industries

| | Share (%) of planning regions where ... is one of the three largest manufacturing industries | | |
|---|---|---|---|
| | Unchanged routinized | Unchanged revolving-door | Unchanged downsizing |
| Chemicals | 16.7 | 25.0 | 10.0 |
| Mineral oil processing | 0.0 | 0.0 | 0.0 |
| Plastics | 0.0 | 0.0 | 0.0 |
| Rubber | 0.0 | 0.0 | 0.0 |
| Stone and clay | 0.0 | 0.0 | 0.0 |
| Ceramics | 0.0 | 0.0 | 0.0 |
| Glass | 0.0 | 0.0 | 0.0 |
| Iron and steel | 0.0 | 0.0 | 0.0 |
| Nonferrous metals | 0.0 | 0.0 | 0.0 |
| Foundries | 0.0 | 0.0 | 0.0 |
| Steel processing | 16.7 | 12.5 | 20.0 |
| Metal construction | 0.0 | 0.0 | 0.0 |
| Machinery | 33.3 | 37.5 | 50.0 |
| Office machinery and computers | 0.0 | 12.5 | 0.0 |
| Motor vehicles | 66.7 | 37.5 | 30.0 |
| Shipbuilding | 0.0 | 0.0 | 10.0 |
| Aerospace | 0.0 | 12.5 | 10.0 |
| Electronics | 50.0 | 100.0 | 70.0 |
| Fine mechanics, watches, gauges | 0.0 | 0.0 | 10.0 |
| Iron and metal goods | 16.7 | 12.5 | 10.0 |
| Jewelry, musical instruments, and toys | 0.0 | 0.0 | 10.0 |
| Wood (excluding furniture) | 0.0 | 0.0 | 0.0 |
| Furniture | 0.0 | 0.0 | 0.0 |
| Paper making | 0.0 | 0.0 | 0.0 |
| Paper processing and board | 0.0 | 0.0 | 0.0 |
| Printing | 16.7 | 0.0 | 0.0 |
| Textiles | 0.0 | 12.5 | 10.0 |
| Leather | 0.0 | 0.0 | 10.0 |
| Apparel | 0.0 | 0.0 | 0.0 |
| Food | 83.3 | 37.5 | 50.0 |
| Beverages | 0.0 | 0.0 | 0.0 |

The quality and availability of *infrastructure* is based on the type of region. The variable can take the values 1, 2 ..., 7, whereby agglomerations are coded 1 and rural areas with less than 2,000 inhabitants are coded 7. Furthermore, the stance local universities and other research institutions take toward the transfer of knowledge to the private sector is measured by the number of patents applied for by the universities and other research institutions.

The availability of differentiated *business services* in a region is measured by the share of employment in business services in the region. A high number of highly qualified employees working in business services indicates the knowledge intensity of those services.

Patent density, measured as the number of patents in a region over the number of engineers and natural scientists in the region, is used as a proxy for the efficiency of regional R&D activities (*inventions*).

Finally, planning regions are characterized by their three largest manufacturing industries, measured by share of employment. The share of employment in large businesses (> 500 employees), the share of engineers and natural scientist in large businesses (> 500 employees), the share of small business (< 20 employees) employment, and the net entry rate within the three *dominant manufacturing industries* characterize the size distribution and dynamics within these industries. Tables 3.4a and 3.4b give an overview of the distribution of the largest manufacturing industries in German planning regions by growth regimes.

## 3.4 Findings

We report our findings along the lifecycle, that is, we start with *entrepreneurial growth regimes*, then move to *routinized growth regimes*, followed by *revolving-door growth regimes*, and end with *downsizing growth regimes*.

Surprisingly, the share of highly qualified employees, as well as the number of engineers, is below average in *entrepreneurial growth regimes*. However, the share of small business employment and the share of bohemians are above average. Creativity and entrepreneurial spirit seem to play a crucial role in entrepreneurial regimes. The number of inventions (patent density) is above average. Knowledge creation takes place in close cooperation between small businesses, independent inventors (patents applied for by natural persons), and business services (share of employment in business services). University knowledge production appears to be of less importance (patents applied for by universities). Dominant manufacturing industries in entrepreneurial growth regimes include motor vehicles, electronics, and food. Industry concentration (employment share of the three largest manufacturing industries) is more or less average, but the share of small business employment in the dominant manufacturing industries is comparatively high. These dominant industries are also characterized by a high net entry rate and are thus dynamic.

*Routinized growth regimes* differ from entrepreneurial regimes in at least three respects. The share of bohemians is below average, which might stem from the fact that routinized growth regimes are more rural (type of region). The number of inventions (patent density) is well above average; however, universities (share of patents applied for by universities) play a more important role in the knowledge production process. Business services (share of employment in business services) have only a subordinated role. Dominant manufacturing industries include motor vehicles, electronics, and a very strong emphasis on food. However, net entry rates in these industries are well below average, which makes them less dynamic than the entrepreneurial growth regimes.

*Revolving-door growth regimes* have a high share of highly qualified employees and engineers, but low levels of small business employment. As revolving-door growth regimes occur in more congested areas (type of region), the number of bohemians and the availability of business services (share of employment in business services) are well above average. However, knowledge production (patent density) is less efficient and most patents are applied for by (large) businesses. Dominant manufacturing industries are mainly focused on electronics, but also include machinery, motor vehicles, and food. These industries are dominated by large businesses and the share of engineers in these large businesses is the highest compared to all other types of growth regime. As these engineers are potential founders of spin-offs, there are high net entry rates in these industries and they are thus dynamic.

In *downsizing growth regimes*, knowledge production is again inefficient and, surprisingly, universities are the most prominent applicants for the few patents that there are. Neither highly qualified employees and engineers nor differentiated business services are available. Dominant manufacturing industries include electronics, machinery, and food. The net entry rate in the dominant manufacturing industries is well below average, making these industries the least dynamic of those investigated.

The above findings lead us to conclude that the outstanding characteristics of dynamic regions in the sense of employment growth and net entry are the simultaneous existence of entrepreneurial spirit, creativity, and dominant manufacturing industries that are small businesses and dynamic. In such regions, the business services available probably concentrate on

providing those services most necessary for young and/or small businesses, for example, financial services. What must be emphasized is that it
is not the *independent* existence of these factors that makes a dynamic region, but that they all occur *simultaneously*. This finding is strongly supported by the fact that in all the other types of regimes studied, one of the
above location factors is missing. *Routinized growth regimes* lack the ability to commercialize their existing creativity, resulting in below-average
net entry, and the employment growth in these regions is predominantly
found in incumbent firms that have a still expanding market. *Revolving-
door growth regimes*, which are dominated by large business structures,
have not much growth in employment, but above-average net entry, possibly due to new business entrants substituting business activities of the incumbents as a result of disaggregation. In *downsizing growth regimes*,
there is neither growth nor creativity; in these shrinking markets, incumbents appear to spend all their energy just holding on to their existent market shares, with none left over for the innovation that might lead to growth.

## 3.5 Implications

Dynamic regions are characterized by the simultaneous presence of several
modern location factors. Different regions are endowed with different mix-
tures of location factors, which largely determines whether they will be vital and growing or stagnant and in decline. For example, big cities have
many more amenities than do more peripheral areas — they possess vital-
ity, many possibilities for social contact, and diversity. They attract new
businesses as it is easy to become part of the existing network. Feldman
(1994a) finds that innovative firms are more likely to settle in areas that
have previously enjoyed innovative success as the region's tacit knowledge reduces the uncertainty of innovative activity. In contrast, peripheral
areas are less densely populated, have fewer businesses, and are less diverse. Furthermore, there are often strong implicit norms operating in peripheral areas that act as a means of social control. These norms can have
the positive effect of creating and maintaining stable and lasting business
structures, but they can also have a negative impact on creativity and innovation, thus creating a less-than-dynamic environment for business growth.

   Several policy implications can be derived from these findings. Cities
are already doing well as far as dynamic growth goes. They already possess many of the factors that attract business and support regional dynamics. Therefore, policy should concentrate on peripheral and underdeveloped regions, perhaps by granting investment subsidies that will make

these areas more competitive and lead to the development of location factors that will invite growth. Doing so will reduce the inequality between different regions and level the playing field when it comes to attracting new business. Investment subsidies are a tried and true way of assisting underdeveloped regions, a way of giving an unattractive area a "facelift" so to speak. However, please note that we do *not* suggest direct interference with firms' location decisions. Individual location decisions are exactly that — individual — and subject to many, many specifics that cannot and should not be influenced by government policy.

Once a business has made its location decision, policy can step in again and aid in developing the type of infrastructure that will attract additional business. If this is done correctly, chances are good that a dynamic and networked region will develop. But what about the losers in the location game? Very often in the past, losers have received a university as a consolation prize, in the hope, one supposes, that a great deal of valuable knowledge will be produced and lead to a thriving environment. This does not happen as these universities often lack focus on leading-edge technology projects and are not sufficiently geared towards diffusing newly created knowledge to the private sector. Knowledge created in a vacuum has no way of escaping. What these losing regions need, instead, is a way of being connected to attractive, vital areas.

# 4 New Business Formation by Industry over Space and Time[1]

## 4.1 Introduction

There is little doubt that new business formation plays an important role in the process of economic development (Fritsch and Mueller 2004; van Stel and Storey 2004; Carree and Thurik 2003).[2] Each new business or market entry represents a challenge to the incumbents and, consequently, may generate significant incentives for improvements. The determinants of new business formation have been investigated theoretically and empirically in a number of ways. Most empirical studies in this field are cross-sectional analyses of different industries or regions.[3] Longitudinal analyses of new business formation processes are rather rare.[4] A severe shortcoming of these analyses is that most of them are limited to only one category of influence – industry, space or time – and tend to neglect other factors. The types of influences that are accounted for is mainly due to the approach chosen. For example, cross-sectional analyses limited to the industry level can only investigate the role of industry characteristics (e.g., minimum efficient size, capital intensity) but not regional determinants such as popula-

---

[1] This Chapter is based on Fritsch M, Falck O (2007) New Business Formation by Industry Over Space and Time: A Multidimensional Analysis. Regional Studies 41: 157-172. Reproduced with kind permission of Taylor & Francis, http://www.informaworld.com.

[2] In this chapter, we use the term "new business" as the overall category for both new firm headquarters and new subsidiaries. Our empirical data include these two categories of new entities.

[3] For an overview of cross-sectional studies of industries see Evans and Siegfried (1994) and Geroski (1995). The evidence of interregional analyses is summarized in Reynolds et al. (1994).

[4] The only longitudinal analyses of new firm formation that we are aware of are Keeble et al. (1993), Johnson and Parker (1996), Sutaria (2001) as well as Sutaria and Hicks (2004).

tion density or workforce qualifications. Without accounting for the regional dimension, however, in the case of such industry-level studies, reliable results cannot be attained if the importance of a certain factor, such as innovation conditions, varies significantly across regions. Additionally, if certain regional conditions stimulate new business formation in some industries but deter start-ups in other industries, the effect of space on the formation of new businesses cannot be adequately assessed by means of an interregional approach that does not account for different industries.[5] Moreover, empirical analyses should include multiple years to control for the possibility that the effect of the different determinants changes over time, and, more particularly, to account for the impact of factors that mainly have an influence on the macro or the national level, such as variation of wages, capital user cost, and overall demand.

As far as we know, such a comprehensive approach which simultaneously analyzes the influence of industry, space, and time on new business formation processes has not yet been conducted, presumably because of limitations in the available data. The available time-series are rather short, differentiation by industry is often rudimentary, and there are hardly any data supporting meaningful spatial categories. This shortcoming may be the cause of the mixed and partly contradictory results that have been found, particularly, in studies across industries (cf. Evans and Siegfried 1994; Geroski 1995). Based on a unique dataset, which was compiled from German Social Insurance Statistics (see Fritsch and Brixy 2004, for details), we use a multidimensional approach to analyze the effects of the three groups of determinants – industry, space, and time – simultaneously. The data cover the period from 1983 to 1997 and provides information on the number of new businesses in each year within 52 private sector industries and 74 regions. The estimates enable us to assess the relative importance of the three types of determinants for new business formation processes. The results should be much more reliable than those found by analyzing only one or two categories of factors.

We begin with a brief outline of the main hypotheses and empirical findings about the determining factors in the decision to set up a business in a certain industry and region (section 4.2). This is followed by an overview of new business formation in West Germany during the period under review (section 4.3). Section 4.4 introduces the basic analytical approach and compares the variation of the number of start-ups over the three analytical dimensions: industry, space, and time. The analysis of relationships is reported in section 4.5. In section 4.6, we discuss the results of our

---

[5] Audretsch and Fritsch (1999) provide some empirical evidence on the industry component of regional new business formation processes.

multi-dimensional analyses. Finally, we draw some conclusions from the analysis, particularly with regard to the merits of the type of multi-dimensional approach applied here (section 4.7).

## 4.2 Hypotheses and Main Empirical Findings

In analyzing new business formation processes, we assume the perspective of a potential founder. According to this "labor market" approach (Audretsch 1995, 47-50; Storey 1994, 60), every member of the workforce is faced with the question of whether to remain in dependent employment (or unemployment) or to start an own business. In this view, the start-up decision is determined by a person's subjective evaluation of the costs and benefits related to these alternatives. One group of factors that may be relevant for this decision is the personal characteristics of the potential entrepreneur.[6] Other factors are characteristics of the industry and of the local environment.

In regard to the qualifications of the potential entrepreneur, many studies find a positive relationship between the education level and the propensity to start a business (Bates 1990). However, work experience, particularly in the industry of start-ups, also seems to play an important role. A stylized fact of interregional analyses of new business formation is that the share of employment in small businesses is conducive to start-up activity (cf. Reynolds et al. 1994). The standard explanation for this result is that working in a small business stimulates the emergence of an entrepreneurial attitude; thus, increasing the likelihood that the businesses' employees will consider starting their own businesses (Beesley and Hamilton 1984; Sorenson and Audia 2000). This interpretation is based on the notion that smaller businesses have a less extensive internal division of labor than do larger businesses; hence, employees of these businesses are likely to gain exposure to a relatively big portion of the often tacit knowledge that is necessary in order to run a firm. This view is supported by evidence from empirical studies showing that many founders worked in small businesses before setting up their own enterprises (Johnson and Cathcart 1979a and b;

---

[6] Individual characteristics which may be conducive to starting a business are an entrepreneurial attitude (the pursuit of economic success, independence, self-realization, and the capability to bear risk), an appropriate qualification (expertise, management abilities) as well as the opportunity costs of becoming an entrepreneur, such as the income and the career prospects provided by the current position (c.f. Chell et al. 1991).

Armington and Acs 2002; Wagner 2004).[7] Moreover, a high level of employment in small businesses in a region is probably associated with a relatively pronounced tradition of entrepreneurship; thereby increasing the confidence of potential entrepreneurs in their ability to open new ventures (Sorenson and Audia 2000, 442f.).[8] This is also the reason why these factors may be somewhat overestimated by the percentage of small business employment because it reflects, to some degree, the historical levels of regional entrepreneurship since most businesses begin small. The relevance of business size structure in a given region in relation to new business formation processes could result from the fact that most founders locate their businesses close to their homes (Johnson and Cathcart 1979b; Mueller and Morgan 1962; Cooper and Dunkelberg 1987). However, the share of employment in small businesses also may be regarded as a proxy for an industry's minimum efficient business size. The smaller an industry's minimum efficient business size is, the fewer the resources that are needed to successfully enter the market are, which makes it more likely that new businesses will emerge in that industry.

An issue related to a potential founder's qualification and minimum efficient size is the technological regime that holds sway in an industry. The concept of technological regime characterizes the nature of innovation activity in an industry, particularly the role of small and large firms (Audretsch 1995, 39-64; Winter 1984). A technological regime is called "entrepreneurial" if a high share of innovation activity is conducted by small firms; whereupon, entrants have a relatively good chance to compete successfully. In a "routinized" regime, the incumbent large firms have the innovative advantage and small firms play only a minor role. Therefore, the survival chances of businesses entering such a market can be assumed to be comparatively small.

Lower levels of capital intensity in an industry mean that less investment is needed to enter the market, which has a salutary effect on start-up activity. Likewise, a high level of new business formation can also be expected in industries with low labor unit costs. Lower levels of capital in-

---

[7] Wagner (2004) found that the propensity to be a nascent entrepreneur is particularly pronounced for employees working in firms which are both small and young. According to Mueller (2006a), work experience in a small firm as well as an entrepreneurial environment has a positive impact on the propensity of someone to be a nascent entrepreneur.

[8] "Through direct contact with successful entrepreneurs, people gain opportunities to gather more information about transition from worker to entrepreneur and to conduct a more accurate personal assessment of their ability to succeed" (Sorenson and Audia 2000, 443).

tensity and relatively high labor unit costs may also indicate industries in which a higher proportion of relevant resources reside in skilled labor rather than being incorporated in equipment. In such industries, highly-skilled employees may face relatively high incentives to exit a business and start their own businesses because they want to appropriate the full value of their skills, which employers tend to underestimate as a result of information asymmetry (Audretsch, 1995). A low level of capital user costs indicates low barriers to entry and should be associated with high start-up rates.

The empirical results concerning the impact of unemployment on new business formation is rather contradictory and unclear. On the one hand, it could be argued that unemployed workers face rather low opportunity costs when starting their own businesses; hence, a high level of unemployment may lead to relatively large numbers of start-ups. On the other hand, high unemployment may indicate relatively low demand and correspondingly bad prospects for a successful start-up. In most of the empirical studies, the impact of the unemployment rate on new business formation was found to be weakly significant or insignificant (cf. Reynolds et al. 1994; Evans and Siegfried 1994; Geroski 1995). A few analyses have found that the percentage change in the number of unemployed had a negative impact on new business formation activity (cf. Reynolds et al. 1994; Sutaria 2001; Sutaria and Hicks, 2004). However, in an analysis on the level of individuals Wagner and Sternberg (2004) found that being unemployed increases the propensity to be a nascent entrepreneur.

There is little doubt that growing demand should be stimulating for start-ups. Yet, it is not quite clear whether the demand for the products of the specific industry or the overall demand is more important in this respect. If the level of start-ups in an industry is related to the stage in its life cycle (Gort and Klepper 1982), then the development of demand on the industry level should be more important.

Another stylized fact of cross-regional analyses is a positive relationship between the level of new business formation and population density.[9] The exact reason for this result is largely unclear because regional density may serve as a proxy for all kinds of regional influences, such as the availability and cost of needed resources like floor space and qualified labor, the presence of specialized services and venture capital[10], spatial proximity to

---

[9] Cf. Reynolds et al. (1994), Fotopoulos and Spence (1999), Armington and Acs (2002).

[10] Sorenson and Stuart (2001) show that spatial proximity between actors may be important for establishing and maintaining a venture-capital relationship. Accordingly, venture capital is not evenly available in all regions.

customers and to other businesses in the industry, the regional knowledge stock and knowledge spillovers (cf. Krugman 1991), quality of life (Pennings 1982) etc. Density may also be regarded as an indicator of innovativeness if agglomerations are characterized by a high level of innovation activity, as is frequently stated in the literature (for an overview see Fritsch 2000). In this interpretation, a positive relationship between density and start-up activity implies that a high level of innovativeness is conducive to new firm formation processes.

## 4.3 Overview of New Business Formation in Germany

Our information on start-ups is generated from the German Social Insurance Statistics (see Fritsch and Brixy 2004, for a description of this data source). The data are comprised of the yearly number of new businesses in the 74 West German planning regions for 52 private-sector industries in the period from 1983 to 1997. Because, the data cover only establishments with at least one employee other than the founder; start-ups of businesses that remain very small without any employees are not included. We exclude new businesses with more than 20 employees in the first year of their existence; as a result, a considerable number of new subsidiaries of large firms contained in the database are not counted as start-ups.[11] Although, the database only includes information at the establishment level; a comparison with information on the regional distribution of headquarters of newly founded firms reveals a rather high correlation, thus allowing our data to also be regarded as an indicator for regional entrepreneurship (see Fritsch and Brixy 2004, and the analyses in Fritsch and Grotz 2002). Planning regions are functional spatial units somewhat larger than labor-market areas consisting of at least one city and the surrounding area (see figure 4.2).[12]

---

[11] The share of new establishments in the data with more than 20 employees in the first year is rather small (about 2.5 percent). Applying a definition without a size-limit does not lead to any significant changes of the results.

[12] The definition of the planning regions developed in the 1980s was used for the whole period for reasons of consistency. For this definition of the planning regions see Bundesforschungsanstalt für Landeskunde und Raumordnung (1987, 7-10). The Berlin region was excluded due to changes in the definition of the region in the time period under investigation. One might suppose that the German unification in 1990 would have had an effect on start-up activity in regions along the former border with East Germany. However, a close inspection shows

According to our data, there were about 126 thousand private sector start-ups per year in the period under examination. Over the years, the number of start-ups increased slightly with a relatively distinct rise between 1990 and 1991. The difference between the average number of start-ups in the 1983 to 1989 and the 1990 to 1997 periods was about 12.3 percent. The majority of the new businesses, about 92.5 thousand per year (73.4 percent of all start-ups), were in the service sector compared to about 14.4 thousand new businesses per year (11.5 percent) in manufacturing.[13] There was an overall trend towards an increasing share of start-ups in the service sector and a corresponding decreasing share in manufacturing sector (figure 4.1). In the service sector, the largest number of new businesses was set up in wholesale and resale trade, hotels and inns, and the non-specified "other" services. In manufacturing, most start-ups were in steel processing, motor vehicles, electrical engineering, furniture, and food (table 4.1).

Not surprisingly, most of the start-ups (52.6 percent) were located in the agglomerations, while only 15.1 percent were in rural areas (table 4.2). The share of new businesses in the service sector was relatively high in agglomerations (76.4 percent) and the lowest in rural regions (67.5 percent). To compare the level of start-up activity between the regions, we also calculated start-up rates by dividing the number of start-ups by the number of employees in a certain industry and region.[14] The average yearly start-up rate (number of new businesses per 1,000 employees) of 7.24 (ta-

---

that such effects, if they exist at all, tend to be rather small and are, in any case, not significant enough to justify the exclusion of these regions.

[13] The "other private sectors" are agriculture and forestry, fishery, energy, water supply, mining, and construction.

[14] Due to the fact that industries and regions differ considerably in their economic potential, the absolute number of new businesses may not be a meaningful indicator for comparisons of new business formation processes. To account for such differences in economic potential, it is a common practice to analyze start-up rates that relate the number of new businesses to an indicator for the economic potential of the respective region. To the degree that new businesses are set up in the industry in which the founder is employed and are located near the founder's residence, the number of employees in an industry and region can be regarded as a measure of the number of potential entrepreneurs. In this case, the start-up rate represents the probability that an employee in a given industry and region will set up a new business during the given period of time (cf. Audretsch and Fritsch, 1994). This interpretation neglects start-ups by unemployed persons. However, there is no plausible way to allocate the unemployed persons to the different industries since information about place of former employment was not available.

ble 4.2) means that per year about every 138th employee started a new business. Generally, start-up rates tend to be higher in the service sector than in manufacturing.

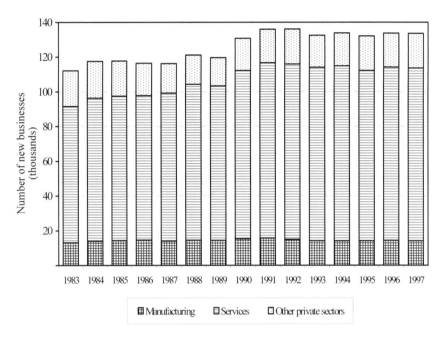

**Fig. 4.1.** Number of start-ups in West Germany per year between 1983 and 1997

Taking the private sector as a whole, we find the lowest start-up rates in the agglomerations. While for manufacturing, the highest start-up rate is in the moderately congested regions, the rural areas show the highest rates for services and other industries. Despite these differences, however, the regional distribution of start-up rates in the two sectors is rather similar to the picture that is produced for all private sectors (figure 4.2). Generally, start-up rates tend to be higher in the northern part of the country but relatively high rates are also found on the western and southern border.

**Table 4.1.** Average yearly number of start-ups in different industries from 1983 to 1997

| Industry | Average no. of start-ups per year (percent share in all start-ups) | No. of regions with zero start-ups in a year |
|---|---|---|
| Agriculture | 7,716 (6.13) | 0 |
| Water, energy | 85 (0.07) | 487 |
| Coal mining | 4 (0.00) | 1,071 |
| Other mining | 19 (0.02) | 928 |
| Chemicals | 177 (0.14) | 267 |
| Mineral oil processing | 7 (0.00) | 1,019 |
| Plastics | 432 (0.34) | 70 |
| Rubber | 45 (0.04) | 692 |
| Stone and clay | 398 (0.32) | 44 |
| Ceramics | 82 (0.07) | 464 |
| Glass | 54 (0.04) | 621 |
| Iron and steel | 15 (0.01) | 946 |
| Non-ferrous metals | 25 (0.02) | 840 |
| Foundries | 53 (0.04) | 660 |
| Steel processing | 1,176 (0.93) | 0 |
| Steel and light metal construction | 655 (0.52) | 26 |
| Machinery (non-electrical excluding office) | 587 (0.47) | 33 |
| Gears, drive units and other machine parts | 360 (0.29) | 75 |
| Office machinery | 35 (0.03) | 755 |
| Computers | 101 (0.08) | 535 |
| Motor vehicles | 1,844 (1.47) | 0 |
| Shipbuilding | 37 (0.03) | 815 |
| Aerospace | 21 (0.02) | 868 |
| Electronics | 1,222 (0.97) | 1 |
| Fine mechanics | 714 (0.57) | 20 |
| Watches and gauges | 31 (0.02) | 796 |
| Iron and metal goods | 493 (0.39) | 53 |
| Jewelry, musical instruments and toys | 230 (0.18) | 239 |
| Wood (excluding furniture) | 111 (0.09) | 376 |
| Furniture | 1,920 (1.53) | 0 |

**Table 4.1.** continued

| Industry | Average no. of start-ups per year (percent share in all start-ups) | No. of regions with zero start-ups in a year |
|---|---|---|
| Paper-making | 12 (0.01) | 945 |
| Paper processing and board | 119 (0.09) | 410 |
| Printing | 775 (0.62) | 24 |
| Textiles | 208 (0.17) | 262 |
| Leather | 260 (0.21) | 159 |
| Apparel | 598 (0.48) | 47 |
| Food | 1,572 (1.25) | 0 |
| Beverages | 68 (0.05) | 548 |
| Tobacco | 2 (0.00) | 1,079 |
| Construction | 6,569 (5.22) | 0 |
| Installation | 4,649 (3.69) | 0 |
| Wholesale trade | 10,519 (8.36) | 0 |
| Resale trade | 20,743 (16.48) | 0 |
| Shipping | 241 (0.19) | 749 |
| Traffic and freight | 6,482 (5.15) | 557 |
| Postal services | 457 (0.36) | 0 |
| Banking and credits | 812 (0.65) | 15 |
| Insurance | 2,051 (1.63) | 0 |
| Real estate and housing | 4,503 (3.58) | 0 |
| Hotels, inns etc. | 16,448 (13.07) | 0 |
| Science, publishing etc. | 4,004 (3.18) | 0 |
| Health care | 7,273 (5.78) | 0 |
| Other private services | 19,296 (15.33) | 0 |

**Table 4.2.** Average yearly number of start-ups in different sectors from 1983 to 1997 by type of region[a]

| Average yearly number of start-ups | Agglomerations | Moderately congested | Rural areas | All regions |
|---|---|---|---|---|
| All private sectors | 66,253 (52.6 / 100) | 40,612 (32.3 / 100) | 18,999 (15.1 / 100) | 125,854 (100 / 100) |
| Manufacturing | 7,169 (49.6 / 10.8) | 4,972 (34.4 / 12.2) | 2,309 (16.0 / 12.1) | 14,450 (100 / 11.4) |
| Services | 50,615 (54.8 / 76.4) | 28,942 (31.3 / 71.3) | 12,816 (13.9 / 67.5) | 92,373 (100 / 73.4) |
| Other industries | 8,469 (44.5 / 12.8) | 6,698 (35.2 / 16.5) | 3,864 (20.3 / 20.3) | 19,031 (100 / 15.1) |
| Start-up rate (number of start-ups per 1,000 employees) | | | | |
| All private sectors | 7.06 | 7.29 | 7.81 | 7.24 |
| Manufacturing | 1.84 | 1.95 | 1.89 | 1.89 |
| Services | 9.41 | 12.82 | 14.89 | 10.87 |
| Other industries | 7.68 | 8.70 | 11.00 | 8.53 |

a: First value in parentheses is row percent, second value is column percent.

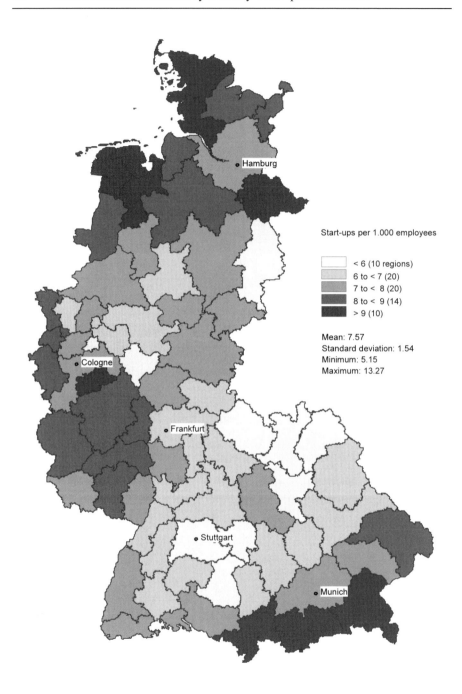

**Fig. 4.2.** Average start-up rates (start-ups per 1,000 employees) in Western Germany for all private sector industries

## 4.4 New Business Formation by Industry over Space and Time

Multidimensional analysis allows different categories of influences to be examined simultaneously.[15] In our approach, these dimensions are industry, space, and time. We analyze to what extent the number of start-ups in a certain industry and region during a certain year is determined by factors that are specific to the respective industries, regions, and years. In doing so, we particularly try to account for interregional differences in industry-specific factors. In the first step of analysis, we break down the total variance of the number of start-ups into three dimensions: industry, region, and time. We estimate the number of start-ups in an industry, region, and year ($y_{irt}$) as

$$y_{irt} = \beta_0 + e_{irt} + u_{ir} + v_r \qquad (4.1)$$

The subscripts $i$, $r$, and $t$ represent the three dimensions of analysis. In our model, dimension $t$ is time (1983-1997), dimension $i$ is industry (52 industries), and dimension $r$ is space (74 West German regions). If an item has all three subscripts $irt$, it varies across all three dimensions. If an item has two subscripts, it varies across two dimensions, and so on. The variables $e_{irt}$, $u_{ir}$, and $v_r$ represent the random variables at the three dimensions, which follow a normal distribution with $E\,(e_{irt}) = E\,(u_{ir}) = E\,(v_r) = 0$ and $var\,(e_{irt}) = \sigma^2_e$, $var\,(u_{ir}) = \sigma^2_u$, $var\,(v_r) = \sigma^2_u$.

The estimation procedure used was iterative generalized least squares. We obtain a value of 33.20 for the constant term ($\beta_0$) in the estimation for the number of yearly start-ups in all private sectors (table 4.3). This gives us the average number of start-ups in an average industry and region during an average year. Restricting these estimations to manufacturing or services resulted in an average number of 5.58 yearly start-ups per industry and region in manufacturing and 104.17 new businesses in the service sector. We found the highest variance for the random variable $u_{ir}$, indicating that the largest part of variation in the number of new businesses is found across industries ($\sigma^2_u$). Considerably less variation could be attributed to region ($\sigma^2_v$), and the smallest share of variation in start-up activity was found over time ($\sigma^2_e$).

---

[15] For a more detailed description of the estimation method see Goldstein (1995), Bryk and Raudenbush (1992) as well as Snijders and Bosker (1999).

**Table 4.3.** Average number of start-ups and estimated variance by industry, region, and over time[a]

| Number of start-ups | Average | Variance by | | |
| --- | --- | --- | --- | --- |
| | | time ($\sigma^2_e$) | industry ($\sigma^2_u$) | region ($\sigma^2_v$) |
| All private sectors | 33.20 (2.94) | 182.65 (1.10) | 7,109.98 (162.37) | 503.64 (104.92) |
| Manufacturing | 5.58 (0.44) | 8.05 (0.06) | 83.48 (2.37) | 12.07 (2.38) |
| Services | 104.17 (10.30) | 556.52 (7.06) | 17,764.38 (882.40) | 6,372.82 (1,293.69) |
| Start-up rate (number of start-ups per 1,000 employees) | | | | |
| All private sectors | 12.93 (0.62) | 1,542.03 (9.62) | 1,287.85 (32.43) | 1.07 (4.72) |
| Manufacturing | 10.08 (0.70) | 2,031.87 (15.59) | 1,077.06 (34.39) | 0.00 (0.00) |
| Services | 18.44 (0.99) | 592.43 (7.58) | 802.93 (41.83) | 1.77 (12.40) |

a: Standard deviation in parentheses

We carried out the same procedure for the start-up rates that account for industry size because the high variation in the numbers of start-ups between industries is to some degree the result of differences in their economic potential. In this case, the smallest amount of variation was found across regions (table 4.3). In manufacturing as well as in the estimates for all private industries, the highest share of variance could be attributed to time. Estimates limited to the service sector showed that industry affiliation was responsible for most of the variation. Obviously, market dynamics play a relatively pronounced role for start-up activity in the service industries. A comparison of the results for the two indicators of start-up activity (i.e., the number of new establishments and the start-up rate) highlights the impact of differences in employment and employment changes on the start-up rate. The higher variance of start-up rates across industry in estimates limited to manufacturing indicates that manufacturing industries differ more with regard to employment than with regard to the number of start-ups. The opposite seems to be the case for the service industries. For all three sector definitions, the variance across regions is much smaller for start-up rates than it is for the number of start-ups. Variation over time is much higher for start-up rates than it is for the number of start-ups. This reflects a considerable impact of changes in employment: the denominator of the start-up rate.

## 4.5 Multivariate Analysis

### 4.5.1 Estimation Procedure

The analysis of the variation of new business formation across the different dimensions showed that the start-up rate was significantly shaped by the change in employment in the respective industry and region (cf. table 4.3). This is one reason why this rate is a questionable indicator in multivariate analyses of new business formation and entrepreneurship over time. Another argument against using the start-up rate in longitudinal analyses is that independent variables with the number of employees as the denominator are affected by employment changes. As a consequence, the estimates for such independent variables may suffer from a positive pseudo-correlation with the start-up rate. In our analysis, this is particularly relevant for the share of employees in small establishments, labor unit costs, and the unemployment rate.[16] For these reasons, we used the number of start-ups instead of the start-up rate as the dependent variable in our analyses of the factors determining new business formation.

Because the number of start-ups which is our dependent variable is of a count-data character we applied negative-binomial (negbin) regression for this analysis. This method is based on the assumption that the counts result from a stochastic poisson-type process. An ordinary negbin regression

---

[16] The analysis by Sutaria (2001) and Sutaria and Hicks (2004) is an example of such a pseudo-correlation when taking start-up rates as the dependent variable. The authors find a positive effect of mean establishment size (mean number of employees per establishment) and the start-up rate, which is defined as the number of new businesses over the number of incumbents. However, if the mean establishment size is relatively high, it causes the number of establishments – the denominator of the start-up rate – to be relatively small, thus, leading to a high value of the start-up rate.

would, however, lead to the problem of having "too many" zero values, which implies a violation of underlying distribution assumptions (see Greene, 2003, 931-939). Given the high degree of regional and industrial disaggregation in our data, such zero-value cases represent a considerable share of all observations. For an analysis across all private sectors, this share amounts to 28.2 percent. In manufacturing it is 34.17 percent and in services the proportion of observations with no start-up in a given industry, region, and year is 10.0 percent. One solution to this problem would be to apply a "truncated" negbin-approach, i.e., to exclude those observations that had no start-ups in a given year. However, because observations with zero start-ups are most likely to occur in industries and regions with a relatively low level of new business formation activity, omission of these observations would lead to a sample that is biased towards large industries and regions with many new establishments. To avoid this problem, we applied a zero inflated negbin approach. This type of model assumes that zero values may result from two different kinds of regimes. Under the first regime, the probability of a positive count (i.e., start-up) in an industry within a certain region is about zero. In this case, a zero observation can, therefore, not be regarded a result of a stochastic poisson process. Under the second regime, the zero observations are assumed to be an outcome of such a poisson process with some positive probability that a start-up in the respective industry and region will occur. The zero inflated negbin approach tries to exclude those zero counts that cannot be regarded to result from a poisson process. This is done here using a logit model with the number of employees in 1,000 employees lagged one year in each industry and region as exogenous variable (cf. Long 1997, chapter 8; Greene 2003, chapter 19.9). In our analysis, we found that the estimates of truncated and zero inflated negbin models were very similar; thus, using one approach instead of the other does not seem to have a significant impact on the results. However, missing values in some of the exogenous variables led to some unavoidable sample bias.[17]

There may be considerable autocorrelation over time because industries and regions with a relatively high number of start-ups in a certain year will tend to have correspondingly high numbers of start-ups in other years. Moreover, an industry population in a region that is characterized by high numbers of start-ups is also quite likely to show comparatively high levels of change in the number of start-ups over time. Such an effect would imply

---

[17] Missing values may occur with regard to the share of small business employment or the entrepreneurial character of the technological regime if there is no employee or no R&D employee present in an industry and region. In our sample, this refers to 1.4 percent of all observations.

heteroscedasticity. Analyses that neglect this cluster-correlated data situation will generally underestimate the true variance and lead to test statistics with inflated type I errors. To avoid these problems, we apply the correction procedure developed by Huber (1967) and White (1980) which provides an unbiased covariance matrix estimator that is robust with regard to this type of heteroscedasticity and autocorrelation over time, even if the model should be incorrectly specified.[18]

## 4.5.2 Variables

Table 4.4 shows the indicators used in our final model for assessing the importance of the different factors on the number of new businesses in a certain industry, region, and year as well as the signs of coefficients that we expect based on the evidence found in earlier studies. While the regional *working population* is an indicator for the pool of potential entrepreneurs, the *share of industry employment* explores as to what extent new businesses are set up by employees of the same industry. The *unemployment rate* in a given region and year indicates the role of unemployed persons in new firm formation activity. We are able to identify the short-term unemployed, which include only those persons which were unemployed for less than one year. Comparing the results of models with the short-term unemployment rate to models with the rate of the longer-term unemployed reveals that the latter has hardly any statistically significant effect on new business formation. This indicates that the short-term unemployed are more likely to set up a new business. Obviously, the longer-term unemployed cannot be regarded as a potential pool of entrepreneurs. Therefore, we include the short-term unemployment rate (share of short-term unemployed persons in the workforce) in the model.

*Small business presence* measured as the share of employees in establishments with less than 50 employees in a given region, industry, and year indicates the role of employment in small establishments as a source of start-ups. Our measure of *minimum efficient size* goes back to Comanor and Wilson (1967, 428) and is quite frequently used in other analyses (see for example Audretsch 1995). Comanor and Wilson argue that the larger-scale establishments of an industry should be relatively efficient because, otherwise, additional smaller units would have emerged. This implies that the smaller establishments are either newly founded or declining busi-

---

[18] Williams (2000) presents a general proof that this estimator is unbiased for cluster-correlated data regardless of the setting.

nesses which suffer from size disadvantages.[19] The indicator for the entrepreneurial character of the *technological regime* measures the importance of small establishments for R&D activity. Note that we calculate the technological regime indicator for each industry in each region separately so that the character of the technological regime in that industry may differ across regions as is suggested by some authors (Saxenian 1994). We find that the indicator for the technological regime highly correlates with indicators that measure the qualification level of the workforce in the industry and region, such as the share of employees with an university degree. One can expect a positive relationship between the qualification variable and the level of start-up activity because the propensity of individuals to set up a new business rises as their level of qualification increases (Bates 1990). In our analyses, estimates with the indicator for the technological regime lead to a better fit than those based on the measures of the qualification level; therefore, we omitted the variables for shares of a certain qualification.

Unfortunately, our information about the number of patents that have been registered by inventors located in a region only covers the years from 1992 to 1994. We use this information to create three dummy variables for the innovativeness of the region. Regions are classified according to the number of patents per 1,000 persons in the workforce in these three years. These dummies are assigned the value zero if the number of patents is in the lower quartile of all regions, and they assume the value one if the number of patents is in the second (patent 25-50), third (patent 50-75), or in the upper quartile (patent 75-100), respectively. This implies the assumption that the level of innovativeness in the regions has remained fairly constant over the period of analysis. The variables *capital intensity, labor unit cost,* and *capital user cost* are important industry characteristics that may show important variation over time. Our indicator for *change of demand* is the percent change of gross domestic product of the respective industry that showed to have a greater impact than the national or regional demand did. In order to account for unobserved region-specific effects, dummy variables for the planning regions have been included. To avoid problems of reversed causality, all independent variables are lagged by one year.

---

[19] Taking the 75th percentile of establishment size is, of course, an arbitrary choice. However, our analyses showed that we get quite similar results for this variable if we chose other percentiles of the size distribution such as the median.

**Table 4.4.** Definition of variables and expected sign of coefficient

| Variable | Operational definition | Expected sign |
|---|---|---|
| Working population | Number of employees and unemployed persons (thousands) in a region and year as an indicator for the pool of potential entrepreneurs (source: Social Insurance Statistics and Federal Employment Services) | + |
| Share of industry employment | Share of the employees in the same industry in the respective region by year (source: Social Insurance Statistics) | + |
| Short-term unemployment rate | Share of persons in a region which are unemployed for less than one year on the regional workforce (source: Federal Employment Services) | + / − |
| Small business presence | Share of employees in establishments with less than 50 employees in a given region, industry, and year (source: Social Insurance Statistics) | + |
| Minimum efficient size | The 75th percentile of establishment size when establishments are ordered by size (number of employees; source: Social Insurance Statistics). | − |
| Technological regime | The proportion of R&D employees in establishments with less than 50 employees over the share of R&D employment in total employment in the respective region, industry, and year (source: Social Insurance Statistics) | + |
| Dummies for regional innovativeness | Three variables based on the number of patents that have been registered by inventors located in a region in the 1992 to 1994 period (source: German Federal Patent Office taken from Greif, 1998) per 1,000 persons in the workforce (source: Social Insurance Statistics). Dummies are assigned the value zero if the number of patents is in the lower quartile of all regions, and they assume the value one if the number of patents is in the second (patent 25-50), third (patent 50-75), or in the upper quartile (patent 75-100), respectively. | + |

**Table 4.4.** continued

| Variable | Operational definition | Expected sign |
|---|---|---|
| Dummies for regional innovativeness | Three variables based on the number of patents that have been registered by inventors located in a region in the 1992 to 1994 period (source: German Federal Patent Office taken from Greif, 1998) per 1,000 persons in the workforce (source: Social Insurance Statistics). Dummies are assigned the value zero if the number of patents is in the lower quartile of all regions, and they assume the value one if the number of patents is in the second (patent 25-50), third (patent 50-75), or in the upper quartile (patent 75-100), respectively. | + |
| Capital intensity | Gross capital assets expressed in terms of 10,000 German marks (source: Federal Statistical Office, Fachserie18, various volumes) over the number of employees (source: Social Insurance Statistics) by industry and year | – |
| Labor unit cost | Gross income from dependent work per employee over gross value added per employee (source: Federal Statistical Office, Fachserie 18, various volumes) by industry over time. | – |
| Capital user cost | Nominal interest rate of ten-year government bonds minus the rate of inflation (source: German Federal Bank, various volumes) plus the average yearly depreciation rate of gross capital assets (based on Federal Statistical Office, Fachserie18, various volumes) within an industry over time | – |
| Change of demand | Percent change of gross domestic product of the industry in the preceding year (source: Federal Statistical Office, various volumes) | + |

We find a considerable degree of spatial autocorrelation in our data; i.e., new business formation processes in adjacent regions are not independent but related in some way. There are two possible explanations for this high degree of spatial autocorrelation. One is that a significant number of entrepreneurs set up a business in an adjacent region. However, this seems quite unlikely given the considerable size of the planning regions and the fact that founders of new businesses tend to locate their businesses in close proximity to their homes (Johnson and Cathcart 1979b; Mueller and Morgan 1962; Cooper and Dunkelberg 1987). A more likely explanation for this spatial autocorrelation is that an entrepreneurial attitude or technological regime influences geographical entities that are larger than planning regions. In fact, Audretsch and Fritsch (2002) found that a certain type of growth regime tends to apply to a larger geographical area. To account for the spatial autocorrelation, an autoregressive error model that includes the weighted average of the disturbance terms of adjacent regions would be appropriate (Anselin, 1988). Such a model has to be estimated by a procedure that maximizes a likelihood function containing these weights. As our dataset contains 52,226 observations (for all private sectors), the weighting matrix for the error terms has the dimension 52,226 x 52,226 and is not computable due to technical restrictions.

To overcome this problem, we apply a spatial cross-regressive model to account for the effects of the adjacent region by including dummy variables for the different Federal States (*Laender*). This type of model has the advantage because it can be estimated with standard estimation procedures. The German Federal States (*Laender)* are also an important level of policy making; hence, this variable may also indicate the effect of policy measures operated at that level. Table 4.5a and 4.5b provide descriptive statistics for the independent variables that have been included into the final model.

Our multidimensional approach, as already stated in the introduction, may give us a clearer picture of the relationships than the analyses which account for only a single dimension. However, the number of dimensions of a certain variable may have an effect on the coefficients. If a variable has only variation over one (e.g., our patent indicator) or two (e.g., labor unit cost) dimensions then the variance is much less pronounced as compared to indicators that vary over all three dimensions. One could, therefore, expect that the impact of variables with variance over less than three dimensions is somewhat underestimated in comparison to indicators that vary over all three dimensions.

**Table 4.5a.** Descriptive statistics of dependent variables[a]

| Variable | Mean | Std. dev. |
|---|---|---|
| | *All private industries* | |
| Working population (in 1,000) (r) | 254.28 | 206.66 |
| Share of industry employment (%) (ir) | 1.88 | 7.57 |
| Share of small business employment (%) (ir) | 50.81 | 32.15 |
| Short-term unemployment rate (%) (r) | 7.86 | 2.30 |
| Industry GDP growth rate (%) (i) | 1.29 | 3.07 |
| Minimum efficient size (i) | 159.59 | 348.23 |
| Technological regime (ir) | 0.71 | 0.88 |
| Capital intensity (1,000) (i) | 1,079.95 | 2,089.71 |
| Labor unit cost (i) | 70.04 | 38.50 |
| Capital user cost (%) (i) | 9.58 | 1.56 |
| Av. yearly n° of patents per 1,000 employees | 1.49 | 0.71 |
| | *Manufacturing and services* | |
| Share of industry employment (%) (ir) | 1.83 | 2.58 |
| Industry GDP growth rate (%) (i) | 1.23 | 3.08 |
| Share of small business employment (%) (ir) | 49.94 | 32.07 |
| Minimum efficient size (i) | 121.73 | 170.89 |
| Technological regime (ir) | 0.72 | 0.84 |
| Capital intensity (1,000) (i) | 1,076.04 | 2,130.54 |
| Labor unit cost (i) | 67.49 | 21.35 |
| Capital user cost (%) (i) | 9.54 | 1.51 |
| | *Manufacturing* | |
| Share of industry employment (%) (ir) | 1.31 | 2.13 |
| Industry GDP growth rate (%) (i) | 0.77 | 3.05 |
| Share of small business employment (%) (ir) | 44.89 | 32.49 |
| Minimum efficient size (i) | 150.56 | 188.16 |
| Technological regime (ir) | 0.68 | 0.74 |
| Capital intensity (i) | 1,102.09 | 2,351.88 |
| Labor unit cost (%) (i) | 70.70 | 19.30 |
| Capital user cost (i) | 10.02 | 0.93 |
| | *Services* | |
| Share of industry employment (%) (ir) | 3.37 | 3.10 |
| Industry GDP growth rate (%) (i) | 2.59 | 2.90 |
| Share of small business employment (%) (ir) | 64.08 | 26.11 |
| Minimum efficient size (i) | 37.63 | 48.33 |
| Technological regime (ir) | 0.82 | 1.09 |
| Capital intensity (1,000) (i) | 1,000.06 | 1,369.95 |
| Labor unit cost (i) | 57.26 | 25.18 |
| Capital user cost (%)(i) | 8.14 | 1.99 |

a: Mean, minimum, and maximum of the mean over time for the dimension in parentheses. i: industry, r: region.

**Table 4.5b.** Descriptive statistics of dependent variables[a]

| Variable | Minimum | Maximum |
|---|---|---|
| | *All private industries* | |
| Working population (in 1,000) (r) | 53.05 | 950.45 |
| Share of industry employment (%) (ir) | 32.95 | 70.94 |
| Share of small business employment (%) (ir) | 0.12 | 100 |
| Short-term unemployment rate (%) (r) | 4.38 | 14.57 |
| Industry GDP growth rate (%) (i) | -5.03 | 9.09 |
| Minimum efficient size (i) | 8.83 | 2,358.21 |
| Technological regime (ir) | 0 | 17.98 |
| Capital intensity (1,000) (i) | 28.13 | 12,600 |
| Labor unit cost (i) | 7.31 | 295.80 |
| Capital user cost (%) (i) | 5.49 | 13.37 |
| Av. yearly n° of patents per 1,000 employees | 0.37 | 3.06 |
| | *Manufacturing and services* | |
| Share of industry employment (%) (ir) | 0 | 27.17 |
| Industry GDP growth rate (%) (i) | -5.03 | 9.09 |
| Share of small business employment (%) (ir) | 0.14 | 100 |
| Minimum efficient size (i) | 9.24 | 975.40 |
| Technological regime (ir) | 0 | 17.98 |
| Capital intensity (1,000) (i) | 28.13 | 12,579.28 |
| Labor unit cost (i) | 7.31 | 124.26 |
| Capital user cost (%) (i) | 5.49 | 13.37 |
| | *Manufacturing* | |
| Share of industry employment (%) (ir) | 0 | 27.17 |
| Industry GDP growth rate (%) (i) | -5.03 | 9.09 |
| Share of small business employment (%) (ir) | 0.14 | 100 |
| Minimum efficient size (i) | 20.97 | 975.40 |
| Technological regime (ir) | 0 | 10.34 |
| Capital intensity (i) | 28.13 | 12,579.28 |
| Labor unit cost (%) (i) | 7.31 | 99.45 |
| Capital user cost (i) | 8.69 | 12.78 |
| | *Services* | |
| Share of industry employment (%) (ir) | 0 | 15.02 |
| Industry GDP growth rate (%) (i) | -3.78 | 6.50 |
| Share of small business employment (%) (ir) | 2.00 | 100 |
| Minimum efficient size (i) | 9.24 | 183.02 |
| Technological regime (ir) | 0 | 17.98 |
| Capital intensity (1,000) (i) | 69.57 | 4,391.66 |
| Labor unit cost (i) | 25.53 | 124.26 |
| Capital user cost (%)(i) | 5.49 | 13.37 |

a: Mean, minimum, and maximum of the mean over time for the dimension in parentheses. i: industry, r: region.

## 4.6 Results

Table 4.6 displays the results of the zero-inflated negbin models for all private sectors. Estimates limited to manufacturing and services taken together, to manufacturing, and to the service industries are shown in tables 4.7 through 4.9. The strong impact of the regional working population on the number of newly-founded businesses clearly indicates the importance of the workforce as a source of entrepreneurs. This variable also stands for agglomeration economies indicating a positive effect of density on new business formation. This finding is also consistent with the hypotheses that emphasize the role of spatial proximity and knowledge spillovers for economic development (cf. Krugman 1991). Due to a high correlation between the number of working population and population density, it is not possible to test for the effect of density with a separate variable in models that contain the size of the workforce. Note that no non-linearities in the relationship between working population and the number of start-ups could be found.

Due to the fact that the coefficients for the share of employment in the industry in which the new businesses are set-up are about as significant as those found for the workforce suggest that a considerable fraction of the founders come from the same industry. Obviously, industry specific qualifications and knowledge plays an important role in many of the new businesses. The results for the short-term unemployment rate indicate that start-ups out of unemployment mainly take place in the service sector. In the estimates limited to start-ups in manufacturing, the short-term unemployment rate is not statistically significant. The share of long-term unemployed persons or a change in the unemployment rate had no significant influence on the number of start-ups.

Our indicator for small business presence (share of employees in small establishments with less than 50 employees) was highly correlated with the measure of minimum efficient size (number of employees representing the 75th percentile of establishments in the industry) as well as with the indicator for the technological regime; therefore, these variables are included in separate models. We found that the indicator of minimum efficient size (model II) had a stronger impact on new business formation than the measure for small business presence (model I).[20] This suggests that the positive relationship between small business employment and start-up activity that has been found in cross-regional analyses may be largely due to

---

[20] This is indicated by the higher t-values of the minimum efficient size indicator as well as by, the in most cases, higher values of the $R^2$ in the models containing minimum efficient size instead of small business presence.

a regional concentration of industries with low minimum efficient size. Our indicator for the technological regime in an industry in a certain location had a considerable impact on start-ups in services and in manufacturing. The positive sign of the respective coefficients clearly indicates that an entrepreneurial character of an industry is conducive to start-up activity. This confirms the results attained by Audretsch (1995) in analyses of a cross-section of industries. In models where the indicator for the technological regime and the measure of small firm presence had both been included, the dominant effect was found for the technological regime indicator. Variables reflecting the formal qualifications of the regional workforce (e.g., share of employees with a university degree) were only significant in models that did not include the indicator for the technological regime. We found considerable correlation between these variables with the technological regime indicator clearly outperforming the qualification measures in models that contained both variables.[21]

Remarkably, in analyses of the data that do not account for regional differences, the indicator for the technological regime of the industry was found to have no statistically significant impact on start-up activity. This suggests that there is an important degree of interregional variation with respect to the character of the technological regime in an industry. A case was made for this by Saxenian (1994) in her comparison of the computer industry along Route 128 and in Silicon Valley. Therefore, analyses on the level of industries that do not account for such regional differences may be misleading.

The level of capital intensity, labor unit cost, and capital user cost were significant with the expected sign. No significant impact could be found for changes of these factors. Change in the gross domestic product (GDP) of the respective industry in the preceding year had a significantly stronger impact than changes in the national figure; consequently, the national GDP change is not included in the models. The estimates show that changes in demand are of significant importance for new businesses set-up in all sectors.[22] The number of patents granted to private firms and other institution (e.g., universities) located in the region represents an overall indicator for the level of regional innovation activity. The results for our measure of re-

---

[21] There is also considerable correlation between the qualification variables and other size related variables such as the share of small business employees and the indicator for minimum efficient size. The reason is that academic qualifications are mainly found in larger firms, not in small ones.

[22] Obviously, this effect is mainly limited to changes in the preceding year because estimate lags for more remote time periods were not found to be statistically significant.

gional innovativeness – regional dummies based on the patent density – signify that a relatively high level of innovation in a region is conducive to start-up activity, particularly for start-ups in manufacturing industries where significance of this variable was higher than for start-ups in the service sector.

If the regional dummies which account for the unobserved region-specific effects are omitted, the coefficients for the technological regime indicator and the regional innovativeness indicator come out to be somewhat larger, but all the other coefficients remain unaffected. The *Laender*-dummies that are supposed to capture the effect of spatial autocorrelation prove to be highly significant; hence, indicating that regions belonging to the same Federal State (*Land*) have things in common. However, the inclusion of this variable for effects of spatial autocorrelation did not lead to any changes in the basic structure of the other influences on the number of start-ups.

There are a number of interesting differences of the determinants of start-ups between manufacturing and the service sector (tables 4.8 and 4.9). The higher value of the coefficient for the working population in services indicates a higher propensity to start a business in this sector. The lower coefficient for the share of industry employment in services suggests that start-ups in this sector require less of an industry-specific knowledge as is the case for new businesses in manufacturing. Also, start-ups out of short-term unemployment seem to play a greater role in services than in manufacturing. We find higher coefficients for capital intensity in manufacturing, whereas the effect of labor unit costs is lower in models limited to the service sector. The indicator of minimum efficient size has greater importance in the service sector suggesting a stronger entry deterring effect of size requirements than in manufacturing. Dummies for industry affiliation and for the years of our observation period have been insignificant if included into our models. These dummies are not contained in the models presented here because of some correlation of these dummies with other variables such as GDP change, unemployment rate, and industry characteristics.

**Table 4.6.** Results for all private sectors

| | I | II | III |
|---|---|---|---|
| Constant | 0.3410 | 3.3055** | 3.4109** |
| | (1.72) | (4.88) | (4.18) |
| Working Population (rt) | 0.0029** | 0.0016** | 0.0029** |
| | (4.05) | (5.63) | (4.23) |
| Share of industry employment (irt) | 0.4157** | 0.3607** | 0.4436** |
| | (4.57) | (4.34) | (4.37) |
| Short-term unemployment rate (rt) | 0.0084* | 0.0179** | 0.0443** |
| | (2.07) | (4.06) | (3.11) |
| Industry GDP growth rate (it) | 0.0081** | 0.0188** | 0.0005 |
| | (5.83) | (5.58) | (0.38) |
| Capital intensity (it) | -0.0001 | -0.0001** | -0.0001* |
| | (0.79) | (2.58) | (2.29) |
| Capital user cost (it) | -0.1220** | -0.1337** | -0.1402** |
| | (5.50) | (5.59) | (3.46) |
| Labor unit cost (it) | -0.0059** | -0.0077** | -0.0281** |
| | (5.32) | (5.59) | (4.11) |
| Share of small business employment (irt) | 0.0320** | - | - |
| | (4.79) | | |
| Minimum efficient size (it) | - | -0.0119** | - |
| | | (5.43) | |
| Entrepreneurial technological regime (irt) | - | - | 0.0317 |
| | | | (1.78) |
| Patent dummies: | | | |
| Patent 25-50 | 0.7989** | 0.9056* | 0.5401* |
| | (4.42) | (2.03) | (2.25) |
| Patent 50-75 | 0.0958 | -0.2423 | 0.6659 |
| | (0.28) | (0.66) | (1.78) |
| Patent 75-100 | -0.2258 | 0.2076 | 0.0319 |
| | (0.75) | (0.93) | (0.12) |
| Chi2 | 23.33** | 9.87* | 12.43** |
| Dummies for planning regions | Yes** | Yes* | Yes |
| Chi2 | (179.19) | (89.62) | (67.71) |
| Dummies for Federal States (*Laender*) | Yes** | Yes** | Yes* |
| chi2 | (25.04) | (19.78) | (17.05) |
| Number of observations | 52,226 | 52,226 | 52,226 |
| ('zero' observations) | (14,731) | (14,731) | (14,731 ) |
| Wald chi2 (26) | 10,454.40** | 7,067.87 ** | 4,842.32** |
| Mc Fadden's R² | 0.173 | 0.178 | 0.132 |
| ML R² | 0.730 | 0.724 | 0.618 |
| Cragg & Uhler's R² | 0.731 | 0.724 | 0.618 |

Zero inflated negbin model with standard errors adjusted for clustering; i: industry, r: region, t: time. Absolute z-statistics in parentheses; **: statistically significant at the 1 percent level, *: statistically significant at the 5 percent level.

**Table 4.7.** Results for manufacturing plus services

| | I | II | III |
|---|---|---|---|
| Constant | 1.0594** | 4.0086** | 4.2013** |
| | (5.06) | (5.55) | (5.76) |
| Working Population (rt) | 0.0030** | 0.0015** | 0.0031** |
| | (4.45) | (5.23) | (5.12) |
| Share of industry employment (irt) | 0.3868** | 0.3242** | 0.3684** |
| | (5.16) | (4.25) | (5.06) |
| Short-term unemployment rate (rt) | 0.0267** | 0.0388** | 0.0782** |
| | (3.73) | (3.61) | (3.53) |
| Industry GDP growth rate (it) | 0.0094** | 0.0221** | 0.0059** |
| | (5.17) | (4.14) | (3.84) |
| Capital intensity (it) | -0.0001 | -0.0001 | -0.0001 |
| | (0.31) | (1.45) | (0.03) |
| Capital user cost (it) | -0.1641** | -0.2141** | -0.2405** |
| | (4.05) | (4.66) | (4.10) |
| Labor unit cost (it) | -0.0102** | -0.0106** | -0.0300** |
| | (5.77) | (4.58) | (5.65) |
| Share of small business employment (irt) | 0.0289** | - | - |
| | (3.75) | | |
| Minimum efficient size (it) | - | -0.0105** | - |
| | | (5.49) | |
| Entrepreneurial technological regime (irt) | - | - | 0.0658* |
| | | | (2.03) |
| Patent dummies: | | | |
| Patent 25-50 | 0.7808** | 1.0576** | 0.5303* |
| | (4.25) | (4.97) | (2.18) |
| Patent 50-75 | 1.0826** | -0.3225 | 0.7728* |
| | (4.07) | (0.87) | (2.02) |
| Patent 75-100 | 0.5885 | 0.1676 | -0.0956 |
| | (1.42) | (0.72) | (0.34) |
| Chi2 | 24.75** | 24.76** | 15.97** |
| Dummies for planning regions | Yes** | Yes* | Yes |
| Chi2 | (149.64) | (84.16) | (73.43) |
| Dummies for Federal States (*Laender*) | Yes** | Yes** | Yes |
| chi2 | (31.62) | (26.41) | (11.90) |
| Number of observations | 48,114 | 48,114 | 48,114 |
| ('zero' observations) | (13,444) | (13,444) | (13,444) |
| Wald chi2 (26) | 8,980.25** | 7,842.03** | 5,138.82** |
| Mc Fadden's $R^2$ | 0.176 | 0.184 | 0.143 |
| ML $R^2$ | 0.732 | 0.732 | 0.644 |
| Cragg & Uhler's $R^2$ | 0.732 | 0.733 | 0.645 |

Zero inflated negbin model with standard errors adjusted for clustering; i: industry, r: region, t: time. Absolute z-statistics in parentheses; **: statistically significant at the 1 percent level, *: statistically significant at the 5 percent level.

**Table 4.8.** Results for manufacturing industries

| | I | II | III |
|---|---|---|---|
| Constant | 0.0076 | 1.7759** | 1.9027** |
| | (0.05) | (4.54) | (5.57) |
| Working population (rt) | 0.0011** | 0.0003 | 0.0009** |
| | (4.86) | (1.45) | (3.97) |
| Share of industry employment (irt) | 0.3613** | 0.2582** | 0.2731** |
| | (6.88) | (6.13) | (4.57) |
| Short-term unemployment rate (rt) | 0.0015 | -0.0099 | 0.0176** |
| | (0.33) | (1.45) | (3.71) |
| Industry GDP growth rate (it) | -0.0011 | 0.0058** | 0.0078** |
| | (1.06) | (5.76) | (6.76) |
| Capital intensity (it) | -0.0004** | -0.0004** | -0.0004** |
| | (4.12) | (5.66) | (4.42) |
| Capital user cost (it) | -0.0756** | -0.0495** | -0.0586** |
| | (4.36) | (4.09) | (7.51) |
| Labor unit cost (it) | 0.0043 | 0.0067 | -0.0068** |
| | (0.26) | (0.19) | (3.81) |
| Share of small business employment (irt) | 0.0207** | - | - |
| | (4.82) | | |
| Minimum efficient size (it) | - | -0.0078** | - |
| | | (5.71) | |
| Entrepreneurial technological regime (irt) | - | - | 0.0993** |
| | | | (3.40) |
| Patent dummies: | | | |
| Patent 25-50 | 1.0031** | 1.4830** | 0.9982** |
| | (5.25) | (7.54) | (4.14) |
| Patent 50-75 | 1.9035** | 2.5146** | 0.5974 |
| | (4.91) | (5.57) | (1.66) |
| Patent 75-100 | 1.5887** | 4.4793** | 0.1944 |
| Chi2 | (4.53) | (5.49) | (0.78) |
| | 32.76** | 112.49** | 19.72** |
| Dummies for planning regions | Yes** | Yes** | Yes** |
| Chi2 | (175.40) | (216.38) | (95.00) |
| Dummies for Federal States (*Laender*) | Yes** | Yes** | Yes* |
| chi2 | (27.16) | (94.37) | (14.21) |
| Number of observations | 35,682 | 35,682 | 35,682 |
| ('zero' observations) | (12,194) | (12,194) | (12,194) |
| Wald chi2 (26) | 2,809.81** | 2,697.35** | 1,459.52** |
| Mc Fadden's $R^2$ | 0.150 | 0.193 | 0.133 |
| ML $R^2$ | 0.562 | 0.635 | 0.505 |
| Cragg & Uhler's $R^2$ | 0.564 | 0.638 | 0.507 |

Zero inflated negbin model with standard errors adjusted for clustering; i: industry, r: region, t: time. Absolute z-statistics in parentheses; **: statistically significant at the 1 percent level, *: statistically significant at the 5 percent level.

**Table 4.9.** Results for services

| | I | II | III |
|---|---|---|---|
| Constant | 0.9242** | 2.7727** | 4.1767** |
| | (3.66) | (5.90) | (5.39) |
| Working population (rt) | 0.0034** | 0.0032** | 0.0009* |
| | (6.87) | (4.31) | (2.04) |
| Share of industry employment (irt) | 0.2352** | 0.1732** | 0.2208** |
| | (4.21) | (4.93) | (4.99) |
| Short-term unemployment rate (rt) | 0.0246** | 0.0191* | 0.0329** |
| | (3.56) | (2.05) | (5.74) |
| Industry GDP growth rate (it) | 0.0083** | 0.0238** | 0.0027 |
| | (3.11) | (6.46) | (0.75) |
| Capital intensity (it) | -0.0001** | -0.0001** | -0.0001** |
| | (4.53) | (4.70) | (5.93) |
| Capital user cost (it) | -0.0166 | -0.0462** | -0.0472* |
| | (1.14) | (3.50) | (2.49) |
| Labor unit cost (it) | -0.0034* | -0.0136** | -0.0100** |
| | (2.01) | (5.65) | (5.51) |
| Share of small business employment (irt) | 0.0282** | - | - |
| | (5.18) | | |
| Minimum efficient size (it) | - | -0.0279** | - |
| | | (7.78) | |
| Entrepreneurial technological regime (irt) | - | - | 0.1027** |
| | | | (4.37) |
| Patent dummies: | | | |
| Patent 25-50 | 0.4669 | 0.6095* | 1.2121** |
| | (1.70) | (2.21) | (3.48) |
| Patent 50-75 | 0.9889** | 1.0571** | 2.0890** |
| | (2.90) | (2.56) | (4.27) |
| Patent 75-100 | 0.3834 | 0.2233 | 3.2427** |
| Chi2 | (1.53) | (0.26) | (4.81) |
| | 12.66** | 24.25** | 23.69** |
| Dummies for planning regions | Yes** | Yes** | Yes |
| Chi2 | (156.66) | (97.89) | (63.95) |
| Dummies for Federal States (*Laender*) | Yes** | Yes** | Yes* |
| chi2 | (38.58) | (24.06) | (17.30) |
| Number of observations | 12,432 | 12,432 | 12,432 |
| ('zero' observations) | (1,250) | (1,250) | (1,250) |
| Wald chi2 (26) | 3,556.28** | 6,490.19** | 3,310.36** |
| Mc Fadden's $R^2$ | 0.132 | 0.150 | 0.097 |
| ML $R^2$ | 0.770 | 0.808 | 0.660 |
| Cragg & Uhler's $R^2$ | 0.770 | 0.808 | 0.660 |

Zero inflated negbin model with standard errors adjusted for clustering; i: industry, r: region, t: time. Absolute z-statistics in parentheses; **: statistically significant at the 1 percent level, *: statistically significant at the 5 percent level.

A number of variables had been tested but did not prove to be statistically significant; therefore, they are also omitted in the models presented in table 4.6 through table 4.9. For example, a variable for the presence of venture capital firms in the region or the share of employees in the banking sector that were meant to represent the local availability of capital had no effect. We also tested a number of interaction terms, particularly, with industry dummies and with the industry GDP growth rate in order to detect differences in the effect of variables over the product life cycle (cf. Agarwal and Gort 2002). However, none of these variables proved to be statistically significant.

## 4.7 Conclusions

Our multidimensional analysis of new business formation in Germany confirmed a number of results from pure cross-sectional studies. We found that the regional dimension plays a key role in new business formation processes; hence, empirical studies may gain important insights by accounting for space. Likewise, studies that focus on regions should be aware of significant differences between industries. Although, the more differentiated data and the higher level of sophistication in the analysis did not substantially contradict the results of previous studies; we were able to shed some new light on a number of issues.

Above and beyond a confirmation of earlier studies, there are at least four results that we find to be particularly interesting. Firstly, we were able to show that it is only short-term unemployment that may have an effect on new business formation while long-term unemployment remained insignificant. This impact of the short-term unemployment rate was, however, only significant for start-ups in the service sector and not for new businesses in manufacturing. Secondly, the positive influence of small business presence on new business formation that has been found in many cross-regional analyses (cf. Reynolds et al. 1994) may, to a considerable extent, be related to the minimum efficient size of the industries that are located in the region. Thirdly, we could demonstrate a significant, positive relationship between the entrepreneurial character of an industry in a certain location and the number of start-ups. This clearly indicates that the characteristics of the technological regime and, therefore, of innovation processes play an important role in the formation of new businesses. The significant link between innovation activities and a considerable part of new business formation processes is also underlined by the positive impact that we find for the level of inventions in a region as measured by dummies based on the number of patents per 1,000 employees. These results clearly indicate that a considerable part of new firm formation is closely related to innovation activity and can be regarded as an important part of the regional (!) innovation system. Fourthly, it is quite remarkable that, although there are some differences between the large economic sectors with regard to certain determinants of new business formation, we found that the same empirical model can be applied to all of the large sectors. This is underlined due to the fact that industry dummies as well as interaction variables of industry dummies with the determinants of new business formation in our model did not prove to be of statistical significance. This indicates that the process of new business formation in the different sectors nearly follows the same principles, although the strength of some determinants may be more or less pronounced in certain industries.

The implications for a policy that wants to stimulate new business formation are straightforward. If, as it has been shown in our analysis, the regional workforce is a main source of new ventures, it would be appropriate to direct policy measures to the potential founders; e.g., trying to raise their entrepreneurial spirit and improve their qualification. According to our results, a considerable part of new business formation processes is linked to innovation activities in the region and constitutes a part of the regional innovation system. Particularly, an entrepreneurial technological regime with innovative small firms seems to be a source and a stimulus for new business formation. A policy aiming at stimulating small business formation could focus on this part of the regional economy. This may involve measures that try to improve technology transfer such as strengthening the network between public research institutions and private sector firms as well as paving the way for innovative spin-offs that may emerge from public research. The strong impact of regional characteristics that we found in our analysis suggests that measures which aim at stimulating new business formation should account for the regional dimension. It could, therefore, be appropriate to involve regional authorities in such a policy or to implement the measures more or less completely at the regional level.

Our analysis has clearly demonstrated that a more disaggregated and differentiated empirical approach may lead to considerable advances in the understanding of reality. Therefore, further research on new business formation processes should take industries and regions seriously and try to account for both of the two dimensions. In an analysis, the main focus should be on the link between start-ups and the level of innovation activity as well as its characteristics in an industry and region. What are the main causal relationships, how pronounced are these relationships, and what does this mean for economic development? Further investigation of these issues should advance our understanding of new firm formation and the process of economic development.

# 5 New Business Survival by Industry over Space and Time[1]

## 5.1 Introduction

Setting up a firm can be an arduous task. Entering a market and competing successfully is subject to severe uncertainty and requires diverse qualifications that are rarely contained in one single person. As a result, a considerable proportion of new firms leave the market relatively soon after entering; thus, in some industries or regions only a minority of the entrants is able to survive for a longer period of time.

Understanding this selection process could contribute considerably to our knowledge about the main determinants that drive the market processes and the development of firm populations. While considerable progress in our knowledge about new-firm formation processes has been made in recent years (cf. Fritsch and Falck 2007), the determinants of success and failure of newly founded businesses are still rather unclear. One main reason for this deficit may be the lack of adequate data for analyzing the development of entry cohorts. A particular shortcoming of nearly all of the available studies is that they do not systematically account for the regional dimension. The results of the empirical analysis presented in this chapter clearly show that regional factors play an important role and add significantly to the explanation of new business survival.

Our analysis of new business survival is based on unique data of yearly start-up cohorts over a 15-year period. The data cover all private sector firms with at least one employee and are available for 52 industries and the 326 West German districts (*Kreise*). We do not know of any other study of

---

[1] This chapter is based on Fritsch M, Brixy U, Falck O (2006) The Effect of Industry, Region and Time on New Business Survival: A Multidimensional Analysis. Review of Industrial Organization 28: 285-306. Reproduced with kind permission of Springer Science and Business Media.

new business survival that was based on such differentiated and comprehensive data. Due to this empirical base, we should be able to identify the influences on the success and failure of newly founded establishments that are specific to the particular industry, region, and period of time much more reliably than other analyses.

We begin with a review of the hypotheses and the empirical evidence on new-firm survival obtained so far (section 5.2). Section 5.3 briefly describes the data, and section 5.4 is devoted to the general survival pattern of the new establishments. The results of the multivariate analysis are reported in section 5.5. Finally, we summarize our main results and draw conclusions for policy as well as for further research (section 5.6).

## 5.2 Hypotheses

Empirical studies have shown that new firms are characterized by a relatively high risk of failure during the first years of their existence. The main reasons for such a *liability of newness* are the problems of setting up an organizational structure and getting the new unit to work efficiently enough to keep pace with their competitors. Another reason for the new firms' relatively high vulnerability to closure is that quite often the firms have to survive a certain time period before the first profit is attained. Some authors assume that older firms also face a relatively high likelihood of closing down. The reason for such a *liability of aging* could be the sclerotic inflexibility of established organizations (*liability of senescence*); an erosion of technology, products, business concepts, and management strategies over time (*liability of obsolescence*); or, particularly in the case of owner-managed firms, problems in finding a successor who is willing to take over the business.[2]

It is commonly assumed that survival rates should be higher in industries where the *minimum efficient size,* which has to be achieved in order to be profitable (Audretsch 1995, 77, 80; Wagner 1994), is relatively small (Audretsch et al. 2000; Tveterås and Eide, 2000). Accordingly, high *capital intensity* in an industry may be expected to hinder the set-up and survival of new firms due to the relatively large amount of resources that is needed for attaining the minimum efficient size (Audretsch et al. 2000; Mayer and Chappell 1992). This may explain the observation that the risk of failure is the lower the larger the initial size of the start-up. If new firms enter the market just barely below the minimum efficient size they may

---

[2] Aldrich and Auster (1986), Brüderl and Schüssler (1990), Carroll and Hannan (2000), Jovanovic (2001), Ranger-Moore (1997).

have less difficulty attaining the breakeven point than do smaller firms. However, distinct barriers to entry such as a large minimum efficient size or high capital intensity could also induce a self-selection process that results in relatively few, but high-quality start-ups with above-average chances of surviving (Dunne and Roberts 1991). Due to such different and contradicting effects, the relationship between the level of entry barriers and new-firm survival rates is a priori unclear (table 5.1).

While a high level of *labor unit cost* and high *user cost of capital* can be assumed to have a negative effect on the success of market entry (cf. Patch 1995, 84), prospering growth in the national economy, in the particular region, or in the same industry may be conducive to economic success and survival (Audretsch 1995, 70-73; Boeri and Bellmann 1995; Rosenbaum and Lamort 1992). However, the relative importance of the different levels is unclear: Is regional prosperity more significant for survival than is national development, or vice versa?

Although innovative industries tend to have above-average growth rates, a high level of *innovative activity* in an industry may make entry more risky; consequently, the effect on new firm survival should be negative (Audretsch 1995; Audretsch et al. 2000; Brüderl et al. 1992). However, new businesses, which are set up in close proximity to innovative firms of the same industry, could also benefit from knowledge spillovers that are conducive to their development (Krugman 1991). For this reason, the effect of an industry's innovativeness at a certain location on the survival of new businesses is undetermined (table 5.1).

The nature of innovation activity in an industry as described by its *technological regime* may be more important than innovativeness itself (Audretsch 1995, 39-64; Marsili 2002; Winter 1984). At an early stage of the industry life cycle, the market is characterized by an "entrepreneurial" regime in which small firms have a high share of innovation activity; thus, entrants face a relatively good chance of competing successfully. A relatively high level of technological turbulence at this stage may, however, imply a high risk and correspondingly high failure rates. Under the conditions of a "routinized" regime – i.e., after the establishment of a dominant design – the incumbent large firms have the innovative advantage. Therefore, the conditions for successful entry and survival in such a market can be assumed to be comparatively unfavorable (table 5.1). The respective empirical evidence is, however, unclear.[3] In this context, it may be impor-

---

[3] While Audretsch (1995) found that new firms have lower survival chances under the conditions of an entrepreneurial technological regime, Agarwal and Audretsch (2001) identify relatively high survival rates in the early stage of the product life-cycle. Better prospects of survival for start-ups under an entrepre-

tant to recognize that considerable differences can exist in regard to the technological regime of a certain industry between regions (see Saxenian 1994, for an illustrative example).[4]

Another factor that may affect the survival chances of new firms is the intensity of competition within an industry or region. This competition can be measured in a number of different ways. One indicator of the level of competition in an industry is the existing number of firms in relation to the volume of demand. The industrial ecology approach (Hannan and Carroll 1992) argues that if the density of firms is relatively high upon a new firm's emergence, this will have a negative impact on the new firm's survival chances.[5] Another indicator of the intensity of competition is the entry rate in an industry or region. A relatively high entry rate indicates intensive competition, which may result in correspondingly high rates of new-firm failure (Audretsch 1995; MacDonald 1986; Sterlacchini 1994). It is, however, unclear whether entry at the national or at the regional level has the greater effect on survival.

The observation that economic activity tends to be clustered in space (Audretsch and Feldman 1996; Cooke 2002; Porter 1998) suggests that certain agglomeration economies are relevant for the location of new businesses and that these advantages compensate for the negative effect of higher cost (e.g. rents, wages) and of competition from other firms located

---

neurial regime are also found by Klepper (2001), Klepper and Simon (2000), and Suárez and Utterback (1995).

[4] In an analysis of new-firm formation in West Germany, Fritsch and Falck (2007) found that the indicator for the character of an industry's technological regime had a much stronger impact when differentiated by region than compared with figures at the national level.

[5] According to this "density delay" hypothesis, organizations that were set up when the industry was crowded have higher rates of exit than do organizations founded in other, less crowded time periods (Carroll and Hannan 1989; 2000). Geroski, Mata, and Portugal (2002, 5f.) provide two explanations for such a phenomenon. The first explanation, called the "liability of scarcity," assumes that organizations created in unfavorable circumstances are in relatively bad shape and less robust. The second explanation suggests that firms that have been set up under crowded market conditions may be pushed into such types of niche where prospects of success are relatively low ("tight niche packing").

**Table 5.1.** Overview of hypotheses about the effect of different factors on new-firm survival chances

| Determinant | Expected sign for relationship with survival chances of start-ups |
|---|---|
| Age | |
| - liability of newness | – |
| - liability of aging (of obsolescence, of senescence) | – / + – |
| Minimum efficient size in industry | – / + |
| Capital intensity | – / + |
| Labor unit cost | – |
| Capital user cost | – |
| Demand growth – national, in specific industry or region | – / + |
| Innovativeness of industry and region | – / + |
| Entrepreneurial character of technological regime in specific industry and region | – / + |
| Early stage of industry life cycle | – / + |
| Market density | – |
| Agglomeration | + (localization or urbanization economies resulting from density or size?) |
| Market concentration | – / + |
| Unemployment | – / + |

in the vicinity. Advantages of setting up a new business in a large agglomeration could include the availability of large, differentiated labor markets and specialized services, easy access to research institutions, the spatial proximity to large numbers of customers as well as to other firms in the industry that may facilitate knowledge spillovers. It is, however, unclear if such advantages result from the proximity to firms that are related to the same industry (localization economies) or to diverse kinds of actors and institutions (urbanization economies). Moreover, such advantages may be more likely to result from the density or the size of a cluster or agglomeration.

The unemployment rate can be an indicator of at least three issues that may be relevant for new-firm survival. First, high unemployment could reflect low growth rates, which may affect the success of start-ups in a positive or negative way (see above). Second, pronounced unemployment results in easy availability of labor and should, therefore, be conducive to the development of new firms. And third, high unemployment can lead to a large share of start-ups created by unemployed persons. This raises the question whether the survival chances of new businesses founded by formerly unemployed persons differ from those of other start-ups. One may, for instance, expect firms founded by unemployed persons to have fewer resources because without employment and regular income, the available amount of capital will be rather limited. Moreover, the qualification level of unemployed persons tends to be below average. On the other hand, if the opportunity cost of a formerly unemployed entrepreneur is relatively low, these founders will not give up a non-successful business easily but will tend to fight until the situation appears hopeless (for an empirical test, see Pfeiffer and Reize 2000).

Table 5.1 provides an overview of the different determinants of new-firm survival and the expected signs for the relationship with new-firm survival.

## 5.3 Data and Measurement Issues

Our information on start-ups and their survival is generated from the German Social Insurance Statistics (see Fritsch and Brixy 2004, for a description of this data source), which covers the vast majority of the private sector in Germany. Since our data comprises only establishments with at least one employee other than the founder, those start-ups that remain very small without any employees are not included.[6] We exclude new businesses with more than 20 employees in the first or in second year of their

---

[6] Start-ups are identified by new establishment numbers in the statistics at a yearly reporting date. If an establishment number disappears, this is regarded a closure. Those short-lived businesses that are set up and closed between two yearly reporting dates are not included in our data. If ownership changes lead to a change of the establishment number, this may be wrongfully identified as "exit" (= disappearance of an establishment number) and "start-up" (= new number). See Fritsch and Brixy (2004) for details.

existence.[7] As a result, a considerable number of new subsidiaries of larger firms, which often begin as a rather large establishment, are not counted as start-ups.[8] Hence, although the data base is limited to the level of establishments, the focus is on entrepreneurship and new firm formation. A detailed analysis of our data base reveals that these data reflect new-firm formation activity relatively well (see Fritsch and Brixy 2004).

We analyze the information about the numbers of newly founded businesses that have been able to survive different time periods. This information is available for the years 1983 to 2000. Because survival rates and hazard rates are logically related, our investigation is equivalent to analyzing hazard rates, i.e. the probability of new business failure in a given time interval.[9] We include only those cohorts of new businesses for which a two-year survival rate can be calculated. Therefore, our information relates to the start-ups from 1983 to 1998. We have this information for every year, differentiated by industry (52 private-sector industries) and region (326 districts or *Kreise*).

We restrict the analysis to West Germany for two reasons. First, information on East Germany, the former socialist GDR, is only available from 1992 onwards – i.e., for a much shorter time period. And second, a number of empirical analyses have shown that economic conditions were rather divergent in eastern and western Germany in the 1990s and that quite different factors governed market dynamics in the two regions (Brixy and Grotz, 2004; Fritsch, 2004). Information about employment and qualification was also taken from the Social Insurance Statistics. Other indicators are based on publications of the Federal Statistical Office (*Statistisches Bundesamt*).

---

[7] The main reason for excluding new establishments with more than 20 employees is that some of the large new establishments reported in our data are probably a result of the reorganization of larger firms and do not reflect the set-up of new establishments.

[8] In our data we are, however, not able to identify if a firm is a subsidiary of a larger enterprise, a headquarter, or a single-plant firm with only one location.

[9] The survivor function S(t) reports the probability of surviving until time t. It gives the probability that failure does not occur before t. The hazard rate h(t) – also known as the conditional failure rate or age-specific rate of failure – is the probability that the failure event occurs in a given time interval if the subject has survived until the beginning of this interval. The hazard rate is completely determined and vice-versa if the survival rate is given. Therefore, the survivor function is nothing else than $S(t) = \exp\{-H(t)\}$ with $H(t) = \int_0^t h(u)du$ being the cumulative hazard function.

The minimum efficient size of an establishment is computed as the 75th percentile of establishment size when establishments are ordered by size (number of employees). This measure goes back to Comanor and Wilson (1967, 428) and is used in other analyses (see for example Audretsch 1995). Comanor and Wilson argue that large-scale establishments are efficient because otherwise, smaller units would have emerged. Accordingly, the smaller establishments are either newly founded or declining businesses that suffer from size disadvantages.

We measure innovativeness by the share of employees in Research and Development (R&D). R&D employees are those with a degree in engineering or a natural science (source: Social Insurance Statistics). The indicator for the technological regime is the proportion of R&D employees in establishments with less than 50 employees over the share of R&D employment in total employment in the same region, industry, and year. This quotient measures the importance of small establishments for R&D activity, thus indicating the entrepreneurial character of a certain industry in a region.[10]

## 5.4 The General Survival Pattern

Figure 5.1 shows the average survival rates of newly founded businesses in the 1984-2000 period. According to the average for all private sector industries, only 80 percent of the start-ups continued to exist after one year. The survival rates are considerably lower in services than in manufacturing. Looking at the hazard rates (figure 5.2), it becomes clear that this higher vulnerability of start-ups in the service sector lasts until the sixth year of their existence. When the first six years are over, the likelihood of going out-of-business is about the same in services and in manufacturing. About 46 percent of the start-ups in manufacturing survived the first ten years compared with about 37 percent in the service industries. Only 25.85 percent of all new service establishments set up in 1984 survived until 2000. In manufacturing this share is about 33.42 percent.

---

[10] This indicator corresponds to the "small-firm innovation rate / total innovation rate" used by Audretsch (1995) as a measure of the entrepreneurial character of an industry. In contrast to Audretsch's indicator, which is based on the number of innovations introduced, our measure refers to R&D input.

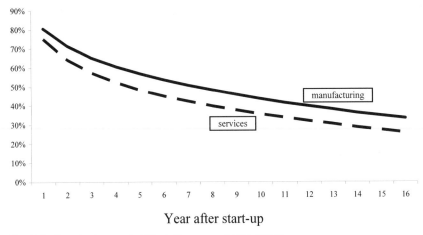

**Fig. 5.1.** Survival rates in West Germany 1984-2000

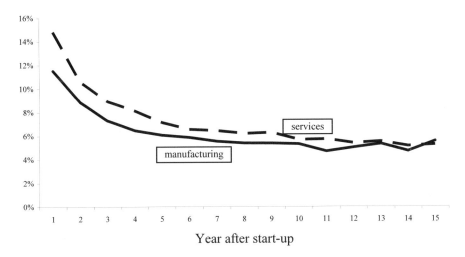

**Fig. 5.2.** Hazard rates in West Germany 1984-2000

There is some variation in the survival and hazard rates over time as shown in table 5.2. While the change in survival rates is somewhat cyclical, there appears to be an increase in the hazard rate after two years and particularly after five years. Pronounced variation in the survival and hazard rates can also be found within the manufacturing and the service sector (table 5.3). The highest ten-year survival rates are in water and energy, fine mechanics, and in health care; by contrast, survival rates are relatively low in hotels and restaurants, apparel, and in agriculture.

The regional distribution of the average five-year survival rate shows a rather mixed picture (figure 5.3). Regions with relatively high survival rates are concentrated in the northern part of Bavaria and Baden-Wurttemberg as well as in the south-east portion of Hesse. The larger cities seem to have low survival rates. This result could be caused by the relatively high share of start-ups in the service sector, which generally tends to have a higher hazard rate (cf. Fritsch and Falck 2007) in these regions. Also, the two-year and the ten-year survival rates tend to be relatively low in agglomerations, while the respective hazard rates are comparatively high (table 5.4). Survival rates are the highest in the moderately congested regions, which represent the middle category between the agglomerations and the rural areas (table 5.4).

**Table 5.2.** Survival and hazard rates for yearly cohorts 1984-1998 after two, five, and ten years

| Year | Survival rate as % after | | | Hazard rate as % after | | |
|---|---|---|---|---|---|---|
| | two years | five years | ten years | two years | five years | ten years |
| 1984 | 60.23 | 46.56 | 35.29 | 10.00 | 5.17 | 5.24 |
| 1985 | 61.69 | 47.96 | 35.55 | 8.54 | 5.55 | 5.29 |
| 1986 | 64.41 | 49.33 | 35.92 | 12.57 | 5.97 | 5.73 |
| 1987 | 63.62 | 50.35 | 36.31 | 8.35 | 6.68 | 6.10 |
| 1988 | 63.99 | 49.58 | 35.44 | 8.79 | 7.01 | 5.15 |
| 1989 | 65.89 | 50.36 | 35.66 | 9.50 | 7.30 | 5.82 |
| 1990 | 65.61 | 49.24 | 34.86 | 10.05 | 7.71 | |
| 1991 | 64.24 | 47.56 | | 10.73 | 7.83 | |
| 1992 | 64.18 | 46.73 | | 11.51 | 7.74 | |
| 1993 | 64.44 | 46.72 | | 11.82 | 7.09 | |
| 1994 | 63.70 | 46.29 | | 12.15 | 7.26 | |
| 1995 | 62.58 | 45.81 | | 12.13 | | |
| 1996 | 62.98 | | | 11.41 | | |
| 1997 | 63.08 | | | 11.91 | | |
| 1998 | 63.72 | | | | | |
| Average | 63.62 | 48.04 | 35.58 | 10.68 | 6.85 | 5.56 |
| Standard deviation | 1.42 | 1.65 | 0.46 | 1.46 | 0.91 | 0.38 |

**Table 5.3.** Average survival and hazard rates 1983-2000 in different industries after two, five, and ten years

| Industry | Survival rate as % after | | | Hazard rate as % after | | |
|---|---|---|---|---|---|---|
| | two years | five years | ten years | two years | five years | ten years |
| Agriculture | 49.51 | 35.39 | 23.16 | 12.94 | 6.33 | 7.90 |
| Water, energy | 77.49 | 64.16 | 56.31 | 4.59 | 3.68 | 12.13 |
| Coal mining | 52.00 | 40.28 | 33.33 | 4.17 | 20.00 | 20.00 |
| Other mining | 65.13 | 42.67 | 28.09 | 11.71 | 8.72 | 10.90 |
| Chemicals | 73.49 | 55.39 | 41.74 | 10.58 | 6.99 | 7.43 |
| Mineral oil processing | 70.42 | 56.12 | 47.57 | 2.98 | 9.09 | 13.89 |
| Plastics | 70.70 | 55.43 | 44.07 | 8.36 | 5.68 | 6.63 |
| Rubber | 72.97 | 60.64 | 49.63 | 7.67 | 4.50 | 5.93 |
| Stone and clay | 73.61 | 61.35 | 48.98 | 7.18 | 4.04 | 3.57 |
| Ceramics | 68.74 | 49.94 | 38.11 | 12.94 | 7.29 | 8.22 |
| Glass | 67.64 | 52.40 | 36.44 | 8.72 | 8.79 | 1.33 |
| Iron and steel | 74.54 | 58.02 | 33.68 | 9.59 | 4.87 | 0.00 |
| Non-ferrous metals | 75.26 | 59.90 | 43.97 | 9.54 | 2.73 | 5.56 |
| Foundries | 71.28 | 55.32 | 42.07 | 9.70 | 3.58 | 4.88 |
| Steel processing | 71.70 | 59.55 | 47.29 | 7.52 | 5.09 | 4.06 |
| Steel and light metal construction | 66.08 | 49.44 | 36.66 | 11.63 | 7.35 | 6.01 |
| Machinery (non-electrical) | 75.26 | 60.58 | 48.48 | 9.79 | 6.24 | 5.24 |
| Gears, drive units other machine parts | 74.20 | 60.39 | 47.18 | 8.19 | 6.02 | 2.85 |
| Office machinery | 71.22 | 54.80 | 41.02 | 10.70 | 4.40 | 2.02 |
| Computers | 70.10 | 52.69 | 35.01 | 10.66 | 8.63 | 6.80 |
| Motor vehicles | 74.46 | 60.74 | 47.37 | 7.97 | 5.58 | 4.13 |
| Shipbuilding | 65.49 | 47.93 | 34.96 | 8.71 | 9.62 | 8.09 |
| Aerospace | 72.90 | 54.44 | 36.17 | 10.59 | 10.14 | 5.71 |
| Electronics | 73.22 | 58.15 | 45.06 | 9.01 | 5.96 | 5.41 |
| Fine mechanics | 82.28 | 72.00 | 58.22 | 5.23 | 4.05 | 4.24 |
| Watches and gauges | 69.88 | 52.95 | 43.49 | 14.43 | 3.74 | 6.55 |
| Iron and metal goods | 72.17 | 58.04 | 46.29 | 7.76 | 5.15 | 6.56 |
| Jewelry, musical instruments, and toys | 68.97 | 54.51 | 40.86 | 9.70 | 7.02 | 7.94 |
| Wood (excluding furniture) | 68.01 | 54.16 | 43.36 | 9.79 | 9.10 | 4.50 |
| Furniture | 70.23 | 56.87 | 44.51 | 8.06 | 5.96 | 5.71 |
| Paper-making | 65.47 | 49.56 | 30.35 | 11.75 | 5.91 | 11.67 |
| Paper processing and board | 70.75 | 56.05 | 41.72 | 9.16 | 6.76 | 5.40 |
| Printing | 70.96 | 57.36 | 43.16 | 8.98 | 6.01 | 5.96 |
| Textiles | 64.33 | 45.49 | 31.57 | 13.91 | 7.25 | 8.85 |
| Leather | 63.99 | 47.56 | 34.14 | 10.76 | 7.58 | 7.17 |
| Apparel | 54.48 | 34.64 | 19.20 | 16.91 | 13.63 | 8.19 |
| Food | 72.37 | 56.76 | 42.99 | 9.41 | 6.78 | 5.83 |

**Table 5.3.** continued

| Industry | Survival rate as % after | | | Hazard rate as % after | | |
|---|---|---|---|---|---|---|
| | two years | five years | ten years | two years | five years | ten years |
| Beverages | 69.07 | 53.47 | 41.65 | 10.13 | 6.42 | 5.71 |
| Tobacco | 43.11 | 15.56 | 4.76 | 0.00 | 10.00 | 0.00 |
| Construction | 57.33 | 40.99 | 30.60 | 14.05 | 8.17 | 6.62 |
| Installation | 73.43 | 60.86 | 48.98 | 7.72 | 5.24 | 4.81 |
| Wholesale trade | 64.22 | 46.87 | 33.01 | 11.43 | 8.53 | 7.21 |
| Resale trade | 63.92 | 47.14 | 33.55 | 11.37 | 7.81 | 6.46 |
| Shipping | 69.30 | 50.18 | 31.11 | 9.96 | 8.41 | 7.31 |
| Traffic and freight | 62.25 | 45.70 | 32.85 | 11.02 | 7.82 | 6.67 |
| Postal services | 68.89 | 53.98 | 42.38 | 15.71 | 18.93 | 16.30 |
| Banking and credits | 65.77 | 48.92 | 36.72 | 11.04 | 7.58 | 5.69 |
| Insurance | 61.76 | 47.50 | 36.91 | 10.09 | 6.22 | 6.14 |
| Real estate and housing | 60.09 | 42.83 | 30.85 | 12.34 | 7.92 | 7.10 |
| Hotels, restaurants etc. | 53.15 | 35.40 | 22.18 | 14.74 | 10.01 | 7.83 |
| Science, publishing etc. | 60.46 | 43.29 | 29.98 | 11.30 | 7.31 | 4.82 |
| Health care | 85.06 | 77.85 | 68.97 | 3.32 | 2.75 | 2.65 |
| Other private services | 68.46 | 53.65 | 41.64 | 9.33 | 6.21 | 4.88 |
| All private industries | 64.13 | 48.53 | 35.87 | 10.62 | 6.92 | 5.75 |

**Table 5.4.** Average survival and hazard rates for cohorts 1984-1998 in different regions after two, five, and ten years

| Type of region | Survival rate as % after | | | Hazard rate as % after | | |
|---|---|---|---|---|---|---|
| | two years | five years | ten years | two years | five years | ten years |
| Agglomerations | 63.42 | 47.49 | 34.83 | 10.87 | 7.11 | 5.78 |
| Moderately congested regions | 64.07 | 48.90 | 36.75 | 10.38 | 6.47 | 5.34 |
| Rural areas | 63.31 | 48.25 | 35.83 | 10.55 | 6.69 | 5.11 |
| All regions | 63.62 | 48.04 | 35.58 | 10.68 | 6.85 | 5.56 |

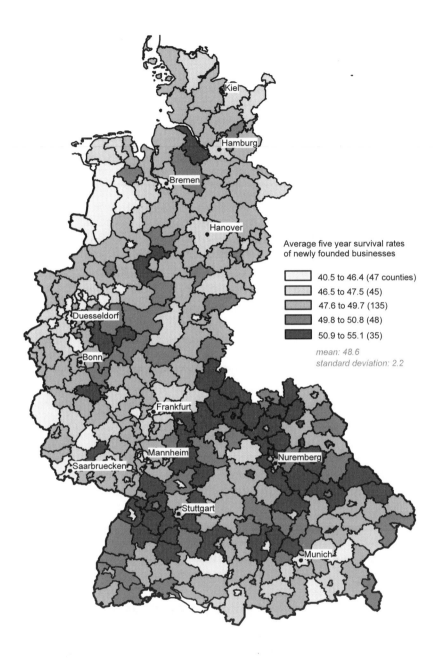

**Fig. 5.3.** Average five-year survival rates (%) in Western Germany 1983 to 2000

## 5.5 Multivariate Analysis

### 5.5.1 Variables and Estimation Procedure

In order to explain the survival rates, we estimated ordinary least square (OLS) regressions applying the Huber-White-sandwich procedure to gain estimates that are robust in regard to autocorrelation over time and hetero-scedasticity between clusters. Heteroscedasticity could particularly occur for the survival rates as a result of differences in the number of start-ups per cell. A Tobit analysis may be more suitable because our dependent variables are rates that have only a limited range of values. This procedure, however, led to almost identical results; hence, we abstain from presenting the respective estimates here. In several cases there were no start-ups in a certain industry, region, and year; thus, these cases could not be included into the analysis because no survival rate could be calculated.

As we mentioned above (section 5.2), density effects could be relevant, and the chances of new-firm survival may not be independent of the level of start-ups in the particular region, in neighboring regions, or in the industry, respectively. Thus, we include the number of new firm entries. Because the number of start-ups may not only be a determinant of survival chances but could also be influenced by the probability of surviving in a certain industry and region, this variable may be correlated with the error term, resulting in biased and inconsistent estimates.

To avoid this problem, we applied an instrumental variables approach, which substitutes the number of start-ups with a variable (the instrument) that is correlated with the number of start-ups but not with the error term. We used the number of employees in the respective industry and region as an instrumental variable for the number of new firms, which has a strong impact on the number of new businesses (Fritsch and Falck 2007). A Durbin-Wu-Hausman test indicated that this instrumental variable approach is not more efficient than including the number of start-ups, and, therefore, the OLS regression is appropriate. We cannot completely exclude that there is also an endogeneity problem with regard to the change of gross value added or with regional and industry employment change in the sense that high survival rates cause correspondingly high growth rates. While it can be regarded unlikely that a regional survival rate has an effect on the change of national GDP or overall employment in the respective industry, it could particularly be relevant in regard to regional employment change. However, we are not aware of any variable that would be suitable to serve as an instrument for these regressors.

If not explicitly noted otherwise, all the values of the explanatory variables relate to the period in which the new establishments started or – in the case of rates of change – to the entire time period under inspection, respectively. Such an approach produced considerably better results than the inclusion of values that relate to a later period of time – e.g., the years shortly before a new establishment closed down. This confirms the analysis of Geroski et al. (2002), who found that the conditions prevailing at the time when new businesses are established have a longer-lasting effect on the firms' survival prospects.

**Table 5.5a.** Descriptive statistics of independent variables[a]

| | All private sector industries | |
|---|---|---|
| Variable | Mean | Std. Dev. |
| Minimum efficient size (i) | 153.22 | 328.94 |
| Share of R&D employees (ir) | 0.02 | 0.04 |
| Technological regime (ir) | 1.28 | 5.30 |
| Sum of start-ups in region and adjacent regions (ir) | 45.07 | 118.23 |
| Population density (r) | 560.67 | 700.18 |
| Growth rate of gross value added | 0.026 | 0.022 |
| Industry employment change (i) | -0.02 | 0.04 |
| Regional employment change (r) | 0.01 | 0.01 |
| Regional unemployment rate (r) | 0.14 | 0.05 |
| | Manufacturing | |
| Minimum efficient size (i) | 144.21 | 176.70 |
| Share of R&D employees (ir) | 0.02 | 0.04 |
| Technological regime (ir) | 0.36 | 0.86 |
| Sum of start-ups in region and adjacent regions (ir) | 8.13 | 13.86 |
| Industry employment change (i) | -0.03 | 0.03 |
| | Services | |
| Minimum efficient size (i) | 36.69 | 45.53 |
| Share of R&D employees (ir) | 0.01 | 0.02 |
| Technological regime (ir) | 4.03 | 10.53 |
| Sum of start-ups in region and adjacent regions (ir) | 148.59 | 204.36 |
| Industry employment change (i) | 0.02 | 0.04 |

a: Mean and standard deviation of the mean over time for the dimension in parentheses. i: industry. r: region.

**Table 5.5b.** Descriptive statistics of independent variables[a]

| Variable | All private sector industries | |
| --- | --- | --- |
| | Minimum | Maximum |
| Minimum efficient size (i) | 9.43 | 2,255.41 |
| Share of R&D employees (ir) | 0 (4,222 cases) | 1 (6 cases) |
| Technological regime (ir) | 0 (2,027 cases) | 121 |
| Sum of start-ups in region and adjacent regions (ir) | 0 (819 cases) | 2,058.73 |
| Population density (r) | 41.35 | 3,984.87 |
| Growth rate of gross value added | -0.022 (1993) | 0.064 (1990) |
| Industry employment change (i) | -0.12 | 0.08 |
| Regional employment change (r) | -0.03 | 0.06 |
| Regional unemployment rate (r) | 0.05 | 0.30 |
| | Manufacturing | |
| Minimum efficient size (i) | 20.51 | 904.89 |
| Share of R&D employees (ir) | 0 (3,164 cases) | 1 (4 cases) |
| Technological regime (ir) | 0 (1,570 cases) | 25.41 |
| Sum of start-ups in region and adjacent regions (ir) | 0 (706 cases) | 131.53 |
| Industry employment change (i) | -0.12 | 0.02 |
| | Services | |
| Minimum efficient size (i) | 9.49 | 172.49 |
| Share of R&D employees (ir) | 0 (992 cases) | 0.30 |
| Technological regime (ir) | 0 (385 cases) | 121 |
| Sum of start-ups in region and adjacent regions (ir) | 0 (28 cases) | 2,058.73 |
| Industry employment change (i) | -0.04 | 0.08 |

a: Mean, minimum, and maximum of the mean over time for the dimension in parentheses. i: industry. r: region.

We performed the analysis for manufacturing industries, for service industries, and for the overall private sector, respectively.[11] Tables 5.5a and 5.5b show descriptive statistics for those variables that have been included in the final model. For all private sector industries, we found the highest minimum efficient size in coal mining and the lowest value in agriculture. Within the manufacturing sector, the maximum value was in the iron and steel industry and the minimum in furniture industry. In the service sector,

---

[11] Note that the overall private sector comprises industries that were not assigned to manufacturing and services such as agriculture, forestry, fishery, energy and water supply, mining, and construction. Therefore, the number of observations in the estimates for manufacturing and services do not add up to the number of observations in models for the whole private sector.

the minimum value was in health care and the maximum value in the shipping industry.

Considerable variation could also be found for the other indicators. There were several cases where an industry did not exist in a certain district or in which the number of employees in the respective industry was rather small. A small number of employees in a certain industry may explain those observations that may appear extreme, such as a 100 percent share of R&D employment. Large differences can particularly be found with regard to the number of start-ups in the industry that occur in a certain region and the adjacent districts. However, such observations are in no way 'outliers' that have any significant effect on the results.

## 5.5.2 Results

Tables 5.6 through 5.8 display the results of our final regression models for explaining the two-, five-, and ten-year survival rates.

The estimations show that spatial autocorrelation is an important issue in explaining new firm survival. We found that the best way of accounting for such neighborhood effects in the model was not only to use the number of start-ups in the respective region as explanatory variable but also to include the number of new businesses that have been set up in the adjacent regions.[12] When start-ups in adjacent regions are included, no other type of exogenous variables for spatial autocorrelation proved to be statistically significant. Running the regressions without border territories where neighboring regions do not exist or are not included in the data set did not lead to any significant changes in the results.

A high minimum efficient establishment size in the industry has a negative impact on new-firm survival in the services sector. Apparently, relatively high hurdles for successful entry into services lead to correspondingly low survival rates. This negative effect of minimum efficient size on new firm survival is particularly pronounced in the estimates for the five-year and the ten-year rates. It takes some considerable time until many of the new businesses attain a competitive size. For start-ups in manufacturing, however, this effect is not statistically significant. This result is surprising given the relatively high values of minimum efficient size in manufacturing (table 5.5). An explanation could be that the higher hurdles for entry in manufacturing induce relatively strong self-selection of entrants

---

[12] The regional number of start-ups and the number of start-ups in adjacent regions are not included as separate variables here but are aggregated to one variable because of a high level of correlation of the values for neighboring regions.

and that this positive impact compensates for the higher problems of attaining a competitive size in this sector. Due to the high share of services sector start-ups, minimum efficient size is also significant with a negative sign in the estimations for all private sector industries.

**Table 5.6.** OLS Regressions of survival rates with robust standard errors, all private industries

| Variables | Two-year survival rate | Five-year survival rate | Ten-year survival rate |
|---|---|---|---|
| Minimum efficient size (it) | 0.0044* | -0.0101** | -0.0156** |
| | (2.15) | (-3.95) | (-5.26) |
| Share of R&D employees (irt) | 0.1846** | 0.1046 | 0.1219 |
| | (4.11) | (1.82) | (1.49) |
| Sum (ln) of start-ups in region and adjacent regions (irt) | -0.0140** | -0.0186** | -0.0179** |
| | (-13.98) | (-14.97) | (-11.79) |
| Population density (r, average over several years) | -0.0161** | -0.0284** | -0.0326** |
| | (-10.29) | (-14.38) | (-14.58) |
| Yearly growth rate of gross value added (average over the period under inspection) | 0.1531** | 0.2712** | 0.1036** |
| | (7.80) | (11.97) | (3.05) |
| Regional employment change (r, average over the period under inspection) | 0.0387 | 0.1260** | 0.1254** |
| | (1.53) | (6.16) | (4.95) |
| Industry employment change (i, average over the period under inspection) | 0.1232** | 0.0066 | 0.1132** |
| | (5.51) | (0.50) | (3.11) |
| Number of observations | 117,448 | 100,386 | 58,466 |
| $R^2$ | 0.184 | 0.208 | 0.203 |
| Durbin-Wu-Hausman test | 6.37 | -0.29° | -2.04° |

i: values per industry. r: values per region. t: per year. *t*-statistics in parentheses. **: statistically significant at the 1 % level. *: statistically significant at the 5 % level. °: The Durbin-Wu-Hausman test is asymptotically valid in conjunction with the robust covariance estimator, but a problem negative test statistics may occur.

The share of R&D employment in the particular industry, region, and year has a significantly negative impact on the survival chances of new businesses in services but proves to be significantly positive for the two-year and for the five-year survival rate in the manufacturing sector. In the estimates for all private sector industries, the respective coefficient is statistically significant only for the two-year survival rate and with a positive sign. The negative coefficients that we find for the share of R&D employment in services industries confirm the hypothesis that entry into innovative industries is relatively risky. We find a significantly positive coefficient for the share of regional R&D employment in the estimates limited to manufacturing start-ups, which demonstrates that there are differences between the large economic sectors. This positive effect may result from the relative prosperity of innovative manufacturing industries that is not perfectly controlled for by the employment change variables in the model. Including the share of R&D employment by year and industry without regional variation leads to considerably lower t-values. This clearly indicates that the regional variation has an effect. Due to high correlation between the share of R&D employment and our measure for the entrepreneurial character of an industry's technological regime, we do not include both variables into the same model. If we substitute the technological regime indicator for the share of R&D employment, it is only statistically significant for the ten-year survival rate in the estimates for all sectors. The respective coefficient shows a positive sign indicating that an entrepreneurial regime is conducive to survival.

**Table 5.7.** OLS Regressions of survival rates with robust standard errors, services

| Variables | Two-year survival rate | Five-year survival rate | Ten-year survival rate |
|---|---|---|---|
| Minimum efficient size (it) | -0.0370** | -0.0860** | -0.1001** |
| | (-7.89) | (-14.09) | (-13.84) |
| Share of R&D employees (irt) | 0.0842 | -0.2572** | -0.4474** |
| | (1.22) | (-2.79) | (-3.42) |
| Sum (ln) of start-ups in region and adjacent regions (irt) | -0.0080** | 0.0191** | -0.0250** |
| | (-5.10) | (-9.60) | (-10.39) |
| Population density (r, average over several years) | -0.0083** | -0.0136** | -0.0208** |
| | (-3.60) | (-4.63) | (-6.20) |
| Yearly growth rate of gross value added (average over the period under inspection) | 0.5372** | 0.6633** | 0.2902** |
| | (17.76) | (19.44) | (6.49) |
| Regional employment change (r, average over the period under inspection) | 0.1164** | 0.0386 | 0.1082** |
| | (3.81) | (1.52) | (4.67) |
| Industry employment change (i, average over the period under inspection) | 0.1287** | 0.0921** | 0.0876** |
| | (4.79) | (6.57) | (3.93) |
| Number of observations | 45,921 | 39,012 | 22,681 |
| $R^2$ | 0.277 | 0.445 | 0.426 |
| Durbin-Wu-Hausman test | 7.87 | 0.01 | 3.25 |

i: values per industry. r: values per region. t: per year. *t*-statistics in parentheses. **: statistically significant at the 1 % level. *: statistically significant at the 5 % level. °: The Durbin-Wu-Hausman test is asymptotically valid in conjunction with the robust covariance estimator, but a problem negative test statistics may occur.

The number of start-ups in the respective industry and region has a negative impact on new-firm survival. As already mentioned above, we also include the number of start-ups in the adjacent regions in this variable, which proves to have an important effect. The highly significant negative sign of the respective regression coefficient obviously reflects the strong competition between a large number of entries and confirms the market density-hypothesis (section 5.2). The start-ups in adjacent regions are obviously the main source of spatial autocorrelation. If start-ups in adjacent regions are included, no other indicator for spatial autocorrelation is statistically significant.

**Table 5.8.** OLS Regressions of survival rates with robust standard errors, manufacturing industries

| Variables | Two-year survival rate | Five-year survival rate | Ten-year survival rate |
|---|---|---|---|
| Minimum efficient size (it) | 0.0039 | -0.0045 | -0.0062 |
| | (1.62) | (-1.54) | (-1.71) |
| Share of R&D employees (irt) | 0.2024** | 0.1561* | -0.0079 |
| | (3.62) | (2.07) | (-0.08) |
| Sum (ln) of start-ups in region and adjacent regions (irt) | -0.0057** | -0.0051* | -0.0079** |
| | (-3.39) | (-2.47) | (-3.05) |
| Population density (r, average over several years) | -0.0183** | -0.0302** | -0.0340** |
| | (-8.80) | (-11.77) | (-11.15) |
| Yearly growth rate of gross value added (average over the period under inspection) | 0.1034** | 0.2194** | 0.1835** |
| | (4.04) | (7.30) | (3.71) |
| Regional employment change (r, average over the period under inspection) | 0.1943** | 0.1622** | 0.1608** |
| | (4.75) | (5.33) | (5.13) |
| Industry employment change (i, average over the period under inspection) | 0.3592** | 0.2760** | 0.2240** |
| | (10.87) | (10.73) | (7.33) |
| Number of observations | 61,441 | 52,769 | 30,777 |
| $R^2$ | 0.164 | 0.193 | 0.156 |
| Durbin-Wu-Hausman test | 0.07 | 9.34 | -22.85° |

i: values per industry. r: values per region. t: per year. $t$-statistics in parentheses. **: statistically significant at the 1 % level. *: statistically significant at the 5 % level. °: The Durbin-Wu-Hausman test is asymptotically valid in conjunction with the robust covariance estimator, but a problem negative test statistics may occur.

The negative relationship between population density and the survival rate of newly founded businesses points towards the relevance of urbanization diseconomies – i.e., negative effects of spatial proximity to economic units affiliated with various industries. This result may also be regarded as an indication of the effect of market density. In order to test for the relevance of localization economies that emerge from the spatial proximity of similar activities, one could include the number of employees in the same industry. Such an approach results in coefficients with a highly significant negative sign. An interpretation of this result is difficult given the considerable statistical relationship between employment and the number of start-ups in an industry (coefficient of correlation of 0.65). The least we can say is that there is no positive net-impact of localization economies on new-firm survival. If spatial proximity to other establishments in the same industry has positive effects on the development of newly founded businesses, these effects may be offset by stronger competition for customers and for resources due to the presence of other suppliers of the same kind in the region.

Change of national gross value added and employment change in the particular industry or region are indicators for the development of demand. We found positive effects for these variables that turned out to be the most pronounced when the change rates were not calculated for single years but for the total life-span of the new businesses.[13] All three indicators show a positive sign, thus indicating that the three dimensions are of some importance. Particularly, the pronounced positive effect of regional employment change indicates that local conditions have an important impact on new business survival even when the national and the industry specific developments are controlled for.[14] The regional unemployment rate in the year when a new business was set up can be regarded as an indicator of two things: the regional economic conditions such as growth rates and availability of labor in that year and the share of new businesses that were founded by unemployed people. Including this indicator in the year when a new business was set up or as an average over the period under inspection in our models did not show any significant effect. We also did not find a stable impact of capital intensity, unit labor cost, and user cost of capital on the survival chances of newly founded businesses.

Dummy variables for industries and years were not included because of their high correlation with many of the explanatory variables. Including dummy variables for certain spatial categories (e.g., high-density agglomeration, rural area) or interacting certain variables with indicators of population density did not result in any significant effects. Conducting the same type of analysis for East Germany leads to a much lower share of explained variance. In contrast to West Germany, we find some considerable variation in new-firm survival rates over time in East Germany (cf. Brixy

---

[13] We did not find any statistically significant impact of growth rates in the year(s) before the particular business was set up.

[14] Including regional employment change in the respective industry instead of the figure for all industries results also in a pronounced positive effect. However, the coefficient is somewhat smaller.

and Grotz 2004; Fritsch 2004). In addition, there are fewer factors that have a statistically significant impact on the survival of new firms, suggesting that survival of new businesses in East Germany is subject to erratic influences to a greater extent than is true in the West. These differences also strongly indicate the importance of regional conditions for the survival of newly founded businesses.

## 5.6 Conclusions

We identified a set of variables that have an impact on the survival chances of new businesses. By simultaneously accounting for the spatial dimension, we were able to show that the regional economic environment is of considerable importance for the success of newly founded businesses. This impact of regional conditions is particularly clear for the number of start-ups in a region, regional innovation activity, regional employment growth, and population density. Moreover, we find pronounced spatial autocorrelation, which also emphasizes the importance of location in terms of 'neighborhood effects'. The impact of a variable always became stronger when it could be disaggregated by region as compared to including the variable without regional differentiation. These findings clearly suggest that empirical analyses of new-firm survival should try to account for the regional level.

If regional factors have an important effect on new business survival, founders are faced with the decision to choose the appropriate location for their start-up. We know, however, from empirical research that founders of new businesses nearly always set up their business close to the place where they reside (Mueller and Morgan 1962; Sorensen and Audia 2000). However, this could also mean that they first settle down in a certain region and then consider whether or not to start a business on their own, often after a considerable amount of time has passed and, perhaps, stimulated by the regional conditions. Given the heterogeneity of industries and new businesses within industries one should be careful in deriving general recommendations for the choice of location from our results. Our results are general trends that should be adjusted to the specific characteristics of a certain project.

There are a number of issues in the analysis that deserve further investigation. First, we should further investigate the ways in which the spatial autocorrelation, which was found in our data, is produced. What are the forces behind these effects? Second, the diverse results that we found for the effect of an industry's minimum efficient size on new firm survival over different time-spans should be further investigated and better understood. Third, the positive relationship between survival in manufacturing industries and the share of R&D employment is still unclear. Finally, it would be desirable to find out the relative importance of the environmental factors as compared to firm specific characteristics. This, however, requires the availability of micro data and information at the level of the respective region and industry.

# 6 Micro-Econometric Survival Analysis of New Businesses[1]

## 6.1 Introduction

It has been said that the great thing about starting your own business is that you get to decide which 24 hours of the day you will work. Maybe it is owner exhaustion that leads to such a high failure rate among new businesses! Joking aside, though, the subject of new business failure has generated extensive empirical research using econometric methods of survival time analysis, covering numerous countries as well as varying time periods. Nevertheless, it is worth revisiting this topic for at least two reasons: First, while industry characteristics are broadly taken into account in micro-econometric survival time analyses, the same is not true of the regional dimension. One main reason for this deficit may be the lack of adequate data for considering the regional dimension. However, if the regional dimension of the data is not considered, estimates may be inefficient and the standard errors may be estimated wrongly due to regional dependency in the error terms.

Second, the results found may be highly country-specific because of different underlying institutions. This chapter aims to provide empirical evidence on the survival chances of new businesses in Western Germany during 1993–2002 using establishment data provided by the Institute for Employment Research (IAB). To date, there is little evidence on new firm survival in Germany due to a lack of micro data with a sufficiently long time series. Although the IAB *establishment panel* is suitable for analyzing the survival chances of new businesses, it has not yet been exploited in this area. Furthermore, the IAB *establishment panel* allows accounting for the regional dimension.

---

[1] A modified version of this chapter is published in *Applied Economics* (Taylor & Francis) with the title *Survival Chances of New Businesses: Do Regional Conditions Matter?*

The remainder of the chapter is organized as follows. Section 6.2 provides a review of the theoretical framework, the hypotheses, and the current empirical evidence on new business survival. Section 6.3 describes the data; section 6.4 discusses the estimation procedure. The results are presented in section 6.5. Finally, section 6.6 sets out a summary of the main results and some suggestions for further research.

## 6.2 Theoretical Framework and Hypotheses

Following Kihlstrom and Laffont (1979), Evans and Jovanovic (1989), and Holtz-Eakin et al. (1994), the entrepreneur's decision to start and continue a business is dependent on the economic profit $P$ from the new business. The profit is defined as

$$P = a(\text{firm-, industry-, regional-level characteristics}) - w \qquad (6.1)$$

where $a$ is the expected accounting profit and $w$ is the wage the entrepreneur could earn in the same industry and region if he or she were to work for someone else.[2] For simplicity, the wage in the industry and region is assumed to be exogenous. The expected accounting profits depend on firm-, industry-, and regional-level characteristics in an uncertain environment. Survival in any time period for any business requires $P \geq 0$.

This simple theoretical framework is in line with empirical studies showing that smaller-scale entry has a lower likelihood of survival than its larger counterparts. Except for Audretsch et al. (1999) and Agarwal and Audretsch (2001), who find that the relationship between firm size and likelihood of survival does not hold for mature stages of the industry life-cycle, most studies found evidence linking start-up size with survival.[3] Aldrich and Auster (1986, 179–183) enumerate four factors for this *liability of smallness* that make survival problematic for small businesses regardless of whether they are new or old, although the major interest in this chapter is in new businesses:

1. The most severe problem facing small businesses is raising capital.
2. Tax laws often work against the survival of small businesses.
3. Government regulation weighs more heavily on small than on large businesses.
4. Small businesses face major disadvantages in competing for labour with larger businesses.

---

[2] Burke et al. (2005) account for the possibility of multi-entrepreneur startups.
[3] For a survey of the literature, see Geroski (1995) and Sutton (1997).

Although the impact of firm size on survival time is widely accepted, the question of whether the initial size of a business or, rather, its current size affects the probability of survival has been answered variously. Mata et al. (1995) found that current size is a better predictor of failure than initial size. Their findings indicate that past business growth matters for survival, suggesting a partial adjustment process for firm size in the postentry period. However, Geroski et al. (2002) found that the conditions prevailing at the time new businesses are set up have a longer-lasting effect on the firms' survival prospects.

Several empirical studies have considered other characteristics of the firm that might have an impact on survival probability, including legal form, foreign property, the affiliation of the business with a multi-unit firm, having a R&D department, and receipt of national subsidies. Whether the new business is a spinoff of an existing business can also be relevant.[4] Many of these variables are closely connected to the size of the business. For example, small businesses can rarely sustain a dedicated R&D department; larger-scale businesses often choose a legal form with limited liability. Therefore, it is still not entirely clear whether business size is the *best* predictor of failure at the firm level, a hypothesis that will be tested later in this chapter.

Technology can have an impact on the size of a business. Industries using technology needs a substantial workforce for implementation will have a high minimum efficient size of establishment (cf. Audretsch 1995, 77–80; Wagner 1994). New businesses, which are frequently set up below the minimum efficient size of establishment, may have difficulty attaining a breakeven point. Therefore, there may be a higher chance of new business failure in industries with a high minimum efficient size of establishment (cf. Audretsch et al. 2000; Tveterås and Eide 2000). Alternatively, Dunne and Roberts (1991) emphasize that high barriers to market entry may result in fewer, but higher-quality, business startups, which will have an above-average chance of success due to a self-selection process.

Phase of the industry lifecycle is also important in the context of business size. According to the seminal papers of Gort and Klepper (1982) and Agarwal (1998), industry evolution is characterized by regularities in the

---

[4] Harhoff et al. (1998) and Mata and Portugal (2002) discuss the impact of legal form on business survival. For more on the influence of foreign ownership, see Hymer (1976), Braconier and Ekholm (2000), Mata and Portugal (2002), and Bernard and Sjöholm (2003). The influence of national subsidies on new business survival is analyzed by Santarelli and Vivarelli (2002). Persson (2004) analyzes the survival chances of businesses that belong to a multi-unit firm. Klepper and Sleeper (2005) discuss the role of spinoffs.

time paths of key industry variables, especially the number of firms or the level of demand. Audretsch et al. (2000) point out that in early phases of the industry lifecycle, standardized products or production procedures are not yet well developed and thus businesses face an above-average risk of failure. In contrast, Audretsch (1995, 65–122) found a positive correlation between probability of survival and industry growth as an indicator for the phase in the industry lifecycle. The rationale for this positive correlation could be that small firms enjoy innovation advantages compared to established larger-scale businesses.[5] Product innovations during the early phases of the industry lifecycle often occur in small firms, possibly as a result of their generally flat organizational structure, which allows a freer and more dynamic flow of ideas unhampered by a rigid management structure.

As the above discussion amply illustrates, *industry* characteristics have received a lot of attention in econometric survival time analyses; however, the same is not true for the *regional* dimension, possibly due to the lack of adequate data. There has been some work in this area, which usually considers macro variables such as national unemployment rate, interest rate, or national gross domestic product (cf. Audretsch and Mahmood 1995). The findings have led to a general expectation that a positive macro-economic development will have a positive influence on new business survival. However, only the analysis by Fritsch et al. (2006) broadly controls for the regional dimension in a survival time analysis using a multidimensional approach.[6] Thus, agglomeration advantages like access to a large differentiated job market, availability of and desire for specialized services, proximity to research centres, and proximity to a large number of consumers can compensate for the negative effects of a particular region's higher costs, wages, or rents (see Audretsch and Feldman 1996; Cooke 2002; Porter 1998). These variables can influence not only the foundation of new businesses, but also their probability of survival. Thus, Fritsch et al. (2006) find that regional characteristics play an important role and that introducing the regional dimension leads to considerable improvement in the estimation results.

---

[5] See Audretsch (1995, 36–64), Marsili (2002), and Winter (1984) for the concept of the technological regime with which innovation activities in industries can be described.

[6] However, there appear to be numerous papers discussing the impact of regional conditions on new firm formation – especially in Eastern Germany – as well as on the development of newly founded businesses. See Steil (1999), Bellmann et al. (2003), Fritsch and Niese (2004), and Brixy and Niese (2004). Fritsch (2005) compares entry and performance of new business in East and West German growth regimes.

Another factor that may affect the survival chances of new firms is the intensity of market competition, which can be measured in a number of different ways. In addition to classical measures of market concentration such as the Herfindahl index, the number of new businesses or the start-up rate in the relevant market can be used as a measure of competition intensity. Mata and Portugal (1994) use the number of firms in the industry as a measure for intensity of competition and find evidence that more competition leads to higher rates of new firm failure. Fritsch et al. (2006) add not only the number of startups in the respective region as an explanatory variable in their multidimensional approach, but also include the number of new businesses started in adjacent regions so as to account for *neighbourhood effects.* They reach the same result — more competition leads to higher rates of new business failure.

Table 6.1 provides an overview of the hypotheses about the effect of different factors on new business survival chances.

**Table 6.1.** Overview of hypotheses on the effect of different factors on new business survival time

| Determinant | Expected sign for relationship with survival time of new businesses |
| --- | --- |
| Business size | + |
| Business growth | + |
| Minimum efficient size in industry | –/+ |
| Early stage of the industry lifecycle | –/+ |
| Economic growth – national or regional | + |
| Agglomeration | + |
| Market concentration | – |

## 6.3 The Survival Pattern of New Businesses in Germany

### 6.3.1 Data

The information on new businesses and their survival is derived from the *establishment panel* (*Betriebspanel*) provided by the Institute for Employment Research (Institut für Arbeitsmarkt- und Berufsforschung, IAB)[7] and contains the results of annual surveys of businesses that have been carried out in West Germany since 1993. The unit of measurement is the "establishment", not the company. The empirical data thus include two categories of entities: firm headquarters and subsidiaries. For the purposes of this analysis, the term "business" is used to describe both types of entity. The population of the IAB *establishment panel* is comprised of all businesses employing at least one employee subject to the compulsory social security scheme. This information is from the German Social Insurance Statistics. Each business with at least one employee subject to social security receives a permanent individual code number that is used to identify the business for purposes of the IAB *establishment panel*. The businesses are selected according to the principle of optimum stratification of the random sample. The stratification cells are defined by ten business size categories and 16 industries. The probability of a business being selected increases with its size; thus the IAB *establishment panel* contains relatively more larger-scale businesses compared to their proportion in the entire population of businesses with at least one employee operating under social security. Figure 6.1 shows the number of businesses included in the sample each year. The businesses participate in an annual questionnaire, conducted by oral interview, that collects information on their characteristics, such as number and qualifications of employees, revenue, and investments. This catalogue guarantees the panel character of the questions and responses. Additional complexes of questions covering, for example, working time flexibility, overtime, and working time accounts are included in selected annual catalogues.

---

[7] See Bellmann (1997) for a description of this data source.

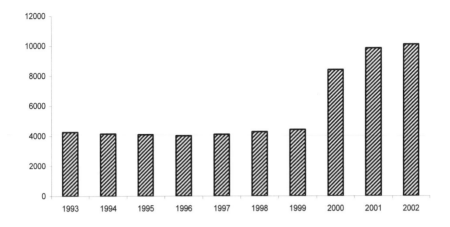

**Fig. 6.1.** Number of businesses included in the IAB establishment panel.
Source: Bellmann (2002, 181)

In this analysis of the survival chances of new businesses, only those
private sector businesses that had been in business for ten years or less at
the time of first questioning were selected from the IAB *establishment
panel*. Although the annual surveys began in 1993, due to mortality and
expansion rates, the beginning year of questioning for the businesses varies. The data is truncated at the left and is also right censored. Businesses
can fail starting from the date of their foundation, of course, but the IAB
*establishment panel* data and characteristics can be observed only from the
time the businesses began participating in the annual surveys, thus creating
left-truncated observation units. Furthermore, not all businesses will fail by
the time of the last considered panel wave. Businesses still in existence at
the time of the last considered wave continue to be at risk of failure, thus
creating right-censored observation units. Both left truncation and right
censoring are taken into account in the hazard function estimation, which
describes the conditioned probability of a business's failure in a time span
$t + \Delta t$.[8] Figure 6.2 demonstrates the Kaplan-Meier hazard function computed on the basis of a nonparametric estimation.

---

[8] For a detailed description of the concept of the hazard function, see section 6.4.

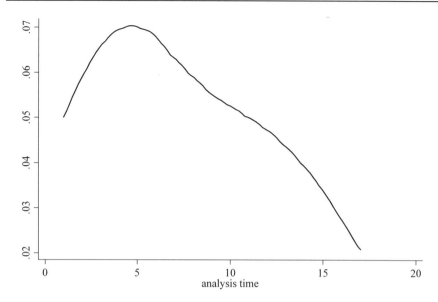

**Fig. 6.2.** Kaplan-Meier smoothed hazard function; analysis time in years
Source: Falck (2007b)

Figure 6.2 reveals a bell-shaped hazard function, with the maximum occurring five years after start up. This high vulnerability to failure in the first few years after start up is referred to in this chapter as the *liability of young adults*. This result is in line with Wagner (1994), who finds, on the basis of data restricted to Lower Saxony, the second largest state of West Germany, that small firms' hazard rates tend to increase during the first years, reach a maximum between the third and fifth year after start up (depending on the cohort being examined), and then decrease nonmonotonically. However, Wagner does not attempt to explain this high *liability of young adults* between the third and fifth year after start up.

## 6.3.2 Liabilities in a Business's Life

Empirical studies have shown that new firms are characterized by a relatively high risk of failure during the first years of their existence. Setting up an organizational structure and experimenting with ways of making the new unit work efficiently enough to keep pace with competitors have been found to be two reasons for this *liability of newness* (cf. Aldrich and Auster 1986; Brüderl and Schüssler 1990).

Furthermore, Brüderl et al. (1992) find a bell-shaped hazard function having its maximum at about 10 months after start up. This *liability of adolescence* is usually explained by the fact that customers and suppliers require a certain amount of time to test and judge the new business's performance.

Older firms can also face a relatively high likelihood of failure. *Liability of aging* could be caused by the sclerotic inflexibility of established organizations (*liability of senescence*); an erosion of technology, products, business concepts, and management strategies over time (*liability of obsolescence*); or, particularly in the case of owner-managed firms, problems in finding a successor who is willing to take over the business (cf. Carroll and Hannan 2000; Jovanovic 2001; Ranger-Moore 1997).

The bell-shaped hazard function found in our data shows a further liability — namely, the *liability of young adults*. The *liability of young adults* results in a hazard function having its maximum at several years after start up, in contrast to the hypotheses of the *liability of adolescence* that results in a bell-shaped hazard function having its maximum much earlier, that is, during the first year of existence.

### 6.3.3 Explaining the Liability of Young Adults

The time-delayed tax-collection process may be one reason for the observed *liability of young adults*. Empirical studies have shown that young businesses tend to be relatively small and that frequently profits are made only some time after starting the business. A hypothetical young business may earn its first profits in the third year after start up. German tax law allows a delay of two years before a declaration of profits must be made, which is then the fifth year after start up. In this year, tax authorities will not only recover the tax due for the third year, but will also demand payment in advance for the fourth year and the current fifth year, the latter on a pro rata temporis basis. Both advance payments are derived from the actual tax due for the third year. Thus, income and business taxes are due for the three consecutive years all at one time.

This triple burden is often insurmountable for young adult businesses — for at least two reasons. First, young adult businesses are still relatively small and have difficulty raising capital. Aldrich and Auster (1986, 179–183) discuss this liability of smallness, which make survival problematic for small businesses regardless of age. Additionally, bank lending policy generally forbids lending money to cover taxes due. Second, in their juvenile carelessness, young adults often make the mistake during their adolescence of not building up reserves for taxes that will come due. When they have finally made their first before-tax profits, overoptimistic young entrepreneurs overconsume in the mistaken belief that the dry spell of business start up is over. Both factors lead to the observable *liability of young adults* occurring several years after start up.

The second factor, in particular, raises an interesting policy-related question: Could entrepreneurship education reduce the observed vulnerability to closure? Parker (2005, 38) states: "It is interesting to speculate that economists might do more good by increasing awareness of the dangers of over-optimistic entry into entrepreneurship than by training gullible starry-eyed MBA students to write business plans that help to lure them to their ruin." In this spirit, further research should attempt to model the behavior of entrepreneurs under bounded rationality and in this way gain insight into designing entrepreneurship education programs that will succeed in improving entrepreneurial skills.

## 6.4 Estimation Procedure

The hazard function introduced in section 6.3 is a common tool in econometric survival time analysis (cf. Lancaster 1990, 6–10). It represents the probability of failure of a business during $t + \Delta t$ under the condition that the business is active up to the time $t$:

$$h(t) = \lim_{\Delta t \to 0} \frac{P(t \le T < t + \Delta t \mid T \ge t)}{\Delta t} = \frac{f(t)}{1 - F(t)} = \frac{f(t)}{S(t)} \qquad (6.2)$$

where $f(t)$ represents the density function, $F(t)$ is the distribution function, and $S(t)$ is the survival function. The survival function is $S(t) = \exp(-\Lambda(t))$ with $\Lambda(t) = \int_0^t h(u)du$ as cumulative hazard function.

In the case of left-truncated and right-censored observations, the likelihood function in general form reads (cf. Kim 2003, 521–522):

$$L = \prod_{i=1}^{N} \left[ \left[ \frac{f(T_i)}{S(E_i)} \right]^{c_i} \left[ \frac{S(T_i)}{S(E_i)} \right]^{1-c_i} \right] = \prod_{i=1}^{N} \left[ h(T_i)^{c_i} \left[ \frac{S(T_i)}{S(E_i)} \right] \right] \qquad (6.3)$$

where $c_i$ is the censoring variable. $c_i$ takes the value one for observation units that fail during the observation period; and zero for observation units still active at the end of the observation period. $E_i$ gives the time of first questioning in the panel. After taking the logarithm, the log-likelihood function results in:

$$\ln L = \sum_{i=1}^{N} \left[ c_i \ln h(T_i) + \ln \left[ \frac{S(T_i)}{S(E_i)} \right] \right]. \tag{6.4}$$

A semi-parametric hazard model, first suggested by Cox (1972), is frequently employed. The covariates $X$ shift the baseline hazard function $h_0(t)$ at each time $t$ proportionally upward or downward depending on influence (cf. Jenkins 2004, 41–44; Hosmer and Lemeshow 1999, 113–115):

$$h_i(t, X_i) = h_0(t) \cdot \lambda_i, \ \lambda_i \equiv \exp(X_i \beta) \tag{6.5}$$
$$\ln(h_i(t, X_i)) = \ln(h_0(t)) + X_i \beta$$

This model is very popular in econometric survival time analyses because the baseline hazard function $h_0(t)$ does not need to be specified. However, very often the strong assumption of the proportional impact of the covariates at each time is incorrect. To test whether the proportionality assumption holds for individual variables in the model or for the entire model, Grambsch and Therneau (1994) suggest computing a test statistic using the Schoenfeld or the scaled-Schoenfeld residuals. For the entire model, the test statistic results in a value of 18.65 ($p$ value 0.0169), which suggests that the proportionality assumption is incorrect, which is also true for the individual variables. Alternatively, an accelerated failure time model can be applied (cf. Jenkins 2004, 44–47; Hosmer and Lemeshow 1999, 271–273). This can be linearized by taking logarithms:

$$\ln(t_i) = X_i \beta + z_i \tag{6.6}$$
$$\ln(t_i \psi_i) = z_i$$

Looking at the second part of equation 6.6, it is obvious that $\psi_i = \exp(-X_i \beta)$ is a time scaling factor that increases the probability of failure and, therefore, decreases survival time for values greater than one. For values less than one, the probability of failure decreases and, therefore, survival time increases. Allison (1995, 62) sets out a helpful example to illustrate this model. As a rule of thumb, one dog life year corresponds to seven human life years. In calendar years, therefore, dogs age faster than humans. Now if $h(t, X)$ is the hazard function of dogs, then $h(t, X = 0)$ describes the hazard function of humans. $\psi$ has the value seven. Thus for $\psi > 1$ the clock ticks faster, for $\psi < 1$ it ticks slower. By differentiating $\beta_k = \dfrac{\delta \ln(t_i)}{\delta X_k}$, it can be shown that the coefficient $\beta_k$ indicates the proportional changes of survival time by changing the value of one regressor by one unit and holding the other regressors constant.[9] $z_i$ is a scaled error term.

The underlying distribution must be further specified for the accelerated failure time model. The bell-shaped form of the hazard function found in the nonparametric estimation suggests a log-logistic distribution for the hazard function in the accelerated failure time model. In contrast to the frequently applied exponential distribution, this distribution has the advantage that in addition to monotonous functional forms, it also permits functional forms like the bell-shaped one found above (cf. Jenkins 2004, 39; Hosmer and Lemeshow 1999, 299–304). A hazard function with a log-logistic distribution is

$$h(t, X_i) = \frac{\psi_i^{1/\gamma} t^{(1/\gamma - 1)}}{\gamma [1 + (\psi_i t)^{1/\gamma}]} \qquad (6.7)$$

where $\psi_i$ is the scaling factor and $\gamma > 0$ determines the shape of the function. For $\gamma \geq 1$, a monotonous falling function results. For $\gamma < 1$, a bell-shaped functional form results. In the model specification set out below, a significant value of 0.5430 results for $\gamma$ (cf. Table 6.4). Further, a graphic presentation of the Kaplan-Meier estimated values of the cumulative hazard function plotted against the model's cumulative Cox-Snell residuals shows that the values are very near the 45° line. This indicates that the model represents the data well (cf. Hosmer and Lemeshow 1999, 303). Only for great values of $t$ is a certain deviation found, which is common for models with right-censored data.

## 6.5 Multivariate Analysis

### 6.5.1 Variables

Prior to setting up the multivariate analysis, the hypothesis formulated in section 6.2 — that business size is the best predictor of failure at the firm level — is tested. In a first step, log-rank or Wilcoxon tests can be used to determine if the survival functions vary for different types of businesses

---

[9] Regression coefficients are interpreted differently in the proportional hazard model. In the proportional hazard model, regression coefficients proportionally shift the hazard rate as the value of one regressor increases by one unit, all other regressors being constant.

(different business sizes, receiving national subsidies or not, having an R&D department or not, being part of a multi-unit firm or not, different types of legal form, being a spinoff or not). The results suggest that most of these characteristics have significant influence on the survival chances of businesses (cf. column (1) and (2) of Table 6.2 for the results and Table 6.3 for the descriptive statistics).

**Table 6.2.** Log-rank and Wilcoxon test for the examination of the equality of the survival functions

| Variable | Log-rank (1) | Wilcoxon (2) | Log-rank Controlled for business size (3) |
|---|---|---|---|
| Business size | 53.22*** | 50.93*** | — |
| National subsidies | 9.87*** | 8.47*** | 0.91 |
| R&D department | 0.60 | 0.99 | 0.01 |
| Part of multi-unit firm | 0.09 | 0.63 | 1.35 |
| Legal form | 3.51* | 3.74* | 1.91 |
| Spinoff | 5.50** | 7.81*** | 1.50 |

* statistically significant at the 10% level; ** statistically significant at the 5% level; *** statistically significant at the 1% level

In a second step, log-rank tests are again carried out, this time controlling for business size. The results show that the difference in survival functions disappears for all firm characteristics considered, suggesting that business size indeed seems to be the best predictor of failure at the firm level (cf. column (3) of Table 6.2).

Based on these findings, only business size and its growth rate are included in the multivariate analysis at the firm level. Additionally, only the size of the business in the examined year can be taken into account here because the IAB *establishment panel* does not include information on the initial size of the business. As discussed in section 6.2, the literature contains different hypotheses regarding the importance of these variables but, due to data limitations, this chapter does not contribute to this debate.

**Table 6.3.** Descriptive statistics of independent variables

| Variable | Mean | Std. dev. | Minimum | Maximum |
|---|---|---|---|---|
| *Business characteristics* | | | | |
| Business size[a] | 101.80 | 456.72 | 1 | 14,421 |
| Employment growth (%)[a] | 10.73 | 81.96 | −100 | 3,500 |
| National subsidies | 1,506 cases (Dummy = 1) | | | |
| R&D department | 400 cases (Dummy = 1) | | | |
| Part of multi-unit firm | 487 cases (Dummy = 1) | | | |
| Legal form (with limited liability) | 1,749 cases (Dummy=1) | | | |
| Spinoff | 800 cases (Dummy = 1) | | | |
| *Industry characteristics* | | | | |
| Employment growth (%)[b] | 0.31 | 2.45 | −3.46 | 4.44 |
| Minimum efficient size[b] | 83.00 | 158.92 | 10.03 | 636.99 |
| *Regional characteristics* | | | | |
| Employment growth (%)[c] | 2.26 | 0.59 | 1.44 | 3.04 |
| Type of region | 0: 28%, 1: 7%, 2: 17%, 3: 8 %, 4: 3%, 5: 2%, 6: 11%, 7:16%, 8: 5%, 9: 3% | | | |
| *Industry x regional characteristics* | | | | |
| Number of new businesses[d] | 1,544.14 | 1,161.19 | 127.81 | 3,784.80 |
| *Macro variables* | | | | |
| GDP growth rate | 1.56 | 0.85 | 0.17 | 2.85 |

a: Mean, minimum, standard deviation, and maximum of the mean over time for the business.

b: Mean, minimum, standard deviation, and maximum of the mean over time for the industry.

c: Mean, minimum, standard deviation, and maximum of the mean over time for the region.

d: Mean, minimum, standard deviation, and maximum of the mean over time for the industry and region.

The following variables are used to characterise the industry and region, as measured at the time of observation:

- Growth rate of employment subject to social security in the industry as a measure of changes in industry demand and, therefore, a proxy for stage of the industry lifecycle (source: Social Insurance Statistics).
- Growth rate of employment subject to social security in the federal state (*Bundesland*) as a measure of regional economic development (source: Social Insurance Statistics).
- Type of region as a proxy for all kinds of regional influences (source: IAB *establishment panel*). The type of region categorizes the municipal-

ity by its density (population + employees subject to social security per square kilometer). The variable can take the values 0, 1, 2, ..., 9. The most populated regions (more than 500,000 inhabitants) are coded 0; regions with less than 2,000 inhabitants are coded 9. This is the only regional indicator in the IAB *establishment panel* that is available for regional units smaller than the federal states.

- Growth rate of the price-deflated national gross domestic product as a measure of macroeconomic development (source: Federal Statistical Office).
- Logarithm of the number of newly founded businesses in the industry located in the respective federal state as a measure of intensity of competition (source: *Establishment file* of the Social Insurance Statistics).
- Minimum efficient size of establishment in the respective industry (source: *Establishment file* of the Social Insurance Statistics). The size of a business refers to the number of persons employed who are subject to social security. The minimum efficient size of an establishment is computed as the average value of 50% of the largest businesses. This method of using size distribution in the industry is based on Comanor and Wilson (1967, 428), who argue that large-scale establishments are efficient business units that profit from size advantages because if there were no advantages to size, multi-unit firms made up of smaller units would have developed. However, there are establishments in the same industry that operate at less than the minimum efficient size. According to Comanor and Wilson (1967, 428), these establishments are either new establishments or establishments that were founded at a time when industry demand was less or technical conditions did not require large units. In addition, smaller businesses can concentrate on market niches.

## 6.5.2 Results

Table 6.4 displays the results of the accelerated failure time model with log-logistic distribution. The covariates in the model are time-variant.

The existing number of employees in the business and the business's employment growth both have a significantly positive impact on the business's survival time. This result agrees with several recent empirical studies showing that smaller-scale entry has a lower likelihood of survival than does it larger-scale entry. Additionally, Mata et al.'s (1995) finding that business growth matters for survival, suggesting a partial adjustment process for firm size in the post-entry period, is confirmed.

The growth rate of employment in the industry, as an indicator for the stage of the industry lifecycle, has a significantly positive influence. The product innovation advantages of small businesses appear to compensate for the high risk of failure in the early stages of industry lifecycle. As industry matures, the probability of new-entry failure increases. Following a suggestion by Agarwal and Gort (2002), interaction terms between the indicator for the stage of the industry lifecycle and all other variables were examined but proved to be insignificant.

**Table 6.4.** Results of the accelerated failure time model with log-logistic distribution; time-varying covariates

| Variable | Coefficient z-value |
|---|---|
| Number of employees subject to social security in business (log) | 0.8135*** 4.01 |
| Growth rate of employment subject to social security in business | 0.0008*** 2.65 |
| Growth rate of employment subject to social security in industry | 0.0287* 1.74 |
| Growth rate of employment subject to social security in federal state | 0.0491** 2.01 |
| Type of region | −0.0523*** −3.93 |
| Growth rate of the price-deflated national gross domestic product | 1.099*** 11.98 |
| Number of newly founded businesses in industry and federal state | −0.1512*** −5.31 |
| Minimum efficient size in industry (log) | −0.1090** −2.22 |
| $\gamma$ | 0.5430 |
| Number of subjects / number of failures | 9,273 / 334 |
| LR $\chi^2(8)$ | 715.77** |
| Log-likelihood | −854.83 |

* statistically significant at the 10% level; ** statistically significant at the 5% level; *** statistically significant at the 1% level

Regional characteristics have an important influence on a business's survival. The type of region and the growth rate of employment in the federal state were two characteristics found to be of significant influence. These regional dynamics, as well as access to differentiated labour markets and proximity to research establishments, suppliers, and a substantial number of consumers, decrease the probability of failure. Or, in other words, these factors significantly increase the chance of business survival over time.

Change in national gross value added, as an indicator of macro-economic development, has a significantly positive effect on the survival time of businesses, a finding in accordance with other studies of macro-economic development using measures such as gross value added growth or unemployment rate.

The number of new businesses in an industry located in the respective federal state has a negative impact on new firm survival. The highly significant negative sign of this coefficient obviously reflects a highly competitive market and confirms the market density hypothesis (Audretsch, 1995).

Finally, startups in industries that have a high minimum efficient size are at higher risk of failure, no doubt because it takes some considerable amount of time before a new business attains a competitive size.

## 6.6 Conclusions

Based on German establishment data, this study identified a set of variables that have an impact on the survival chances of new businesses, an important contribution to this field of inquiry as there has not been much work done on this subject regarding the German situation. By simultaneously accounting for three dimensions (firm, industry, and region) of new business survival, the chapter illustrates the remarkable importance of the regional dimension, a dimension rarely considered to date. The regional characteristics that have the largest impact on new firm survival include the number of new businesses in the relevant regional market, regional employment growth, and the size of the region. The findings are particularly relevant in demonstrating that failure to consider regional characteristics in similar research may cause inefficient estimates due to spatial dependency of the error terms.

Also brought to light is the fact that, aside from business size and business growth, a business's internal characteristics have no bearing on risk of failure. This rather surprising result appears to imply that business size is indeed the best predictor of failure at the firm level.

This study answered some questions, but raised a few new ones as well. Future investigations would most usefully add to the body of knowledge by describing the regional dimension in more detail and dividing it into smaller units. This would achieve a better understanding of the relative importance of the different regional influences. However, and as a note of caution, dividing the regional dimension into smaller units, the problems of spatial autocorrelation and spatial spillovers will become more pronounced, thus necessitating the use of spatial econometric methods. Furthermore, the predominant role of the business size as the best predictor of failure at the firm level is worth a deeper investigation. In doing this, it is required to look inside the firm which opens the floor for a fruitful cooperation between economics and management science.

# References

Abernathy F, Dunlop J, Hammond J, Weil D (1999) A Stitch in Time. Oxford University Press, New York

Acemoglu D (2002) Technical Change, Inequality, and the Labor Market. Journal of Economic Literature 40: 7–72

Acs ZJ, Audretsch DB, Braunerhjelm P, Carlsson B (2004) The Missing Link: The Knowledge Filter and Entrepreneurship in Endogenous Growth. CEPR Discussion Paper 4783

Agarwal R (1998) Evolutionary Trends of Industry Variables. International Journal of Industrial Organization 16: 511–525

Agarwal R, Audretsch DB (2001) Does Entry Size Matter? The Impact of the Life Cycle and Technology on Firm Survival. Journal of Industrial Economics 49: 21–42

Agarwal R, Gort M (2002) Firm and Product Life Cycles and Firm Survival. American Economic Review 92: 184–190

Aghion P, Blundell R, Griffith R, Howitt P, Prantl S (2004) Entry and Productivity Growth: Evidence from Micro-Level Panel Data. Journal of the European Economic Association, Papers and Proceedings 2: 265-276

Aghion P, Burgess R, Redding S, Zilibotti F (2005) Entry Liberalization and Inequality in Industrial Performance. Journal of the European Economic Association, Papers and Proceedings 3: 291-302

Aghion P, Howitt P (2006) Joseph Schumpeter Lecture — Appropriate Growth Policy: A Unifying Framework. Journal of the European Economic Association 4: 269–314

Aldrich HE, Auster ER (1986) Even Dwarfs Started Small: Liabilities of Size and Age and their Strategic Implications. Research in Organizational Behavior 8, 165-198

Allison PD (1995) Survival Analysis Using the SAS System: A Practical Guide. SAS Institute

Anselin L (1988) Spatial Econometrics: Methods and Models. Kluwer Academic Publisher, Dordrecht

Armington C, Acs ZJ (2002) The Determinants of Regional Variation in New Firm Formation. Regional Studies 36: 33-45

Audretsch DB (1995) Innovation and Industry Evolution. MIT Press, Cambridge, MA

Audretsch DB, Feldman M (1996) Knowledge spillovers and the geography of innovation and production. American Economic Review: 86: 630-640

Audretsch DB, Feldman M (2004) Knowledge Spillovers and the Geography of Innovation. In: Handbook of Urban and Regional Economics 4, pp. 2713–2739

Audretsch DB, Fritsch M (1994) On the Measurement of Entry Rates. Empirica 21: 105-113

Audretsch DB, Fritsch M (1999) The Industry Component of Regional New Firm Formation Processes. Review of Industrial Organization 15: 239-252

Audretsch DB, Fritsch M (2002) Growth Regimes Over Time and Space. Regional Studies 36: 113–124

Audretsch DB, Houweling P, Thurik AR (2000) Firm Survival in the Netherlands. Review of Industrial Organization 16: 1-11

Audretsch DB, Mahmood T (1995) The Rate of Hazard Confronting New Firms and Plants in U.S. Manufacturing. Review of Industrial Organization 9: 41–56

Audretsch DB, Santarelli E, Vivarelli M (1999) Start-Up Size and Industrial Dynamics: Some Evidence from Italian Manufacturing. International Journal of Industrial Organization 17: 965–983

Bates T (1990) Entrepreneur Human Capital Inputs and Small Business Longevity. Review of Economics and Statistics 72: 551-559

Baumol WJ, Panzar JC, Willig RD (1982) Contestable Markets and the Theory of Industry Structure. Harcourt Brace Jovanovic, New York

Beck N (2001) Time-Series-Cross-Section Data. Statistica Neerlandica 55: 111–133

Beesley ME, Hamilton RT (1984) Small firms' seedbed role and the concept of turbulence. Journal of Industrial Economics 33: 217-231

Bellmann L (1997) The IAB Establishment Panel with an Exemplary Analysis of Employment Expectations. IAB Labour Market Research Topics 20

Bellmann L (2002) Das IAB-Betriebspanel: Konzeption und Anwendungsbereiche. Allgemeines Statistisches Archiv 86: 177–188

Bellmann L, Bernien M, Kölling A, Möller I, Wahse J (2003) Arbeitsplatzdynamik in betrieblichen Neugründungen Ostdeutschlands. BeitrAB 268, Nürnberg

Bernard AB, Sjöholm F (2003) Foreign Owners and Plant Survival. NBER Working Paper 10039

Boeri T, Bellmann L (1995) Post-entry behaviour and the cycle: Evidence from Germany. International Journal of Industrial Organization 13: 483-500

Braconier H, Ekholm K (2000) Swedish Multinational and Competition from High and Low Wage Locations. Review of International Economics 8: 448–461

Brixy U, Grotz R (2004) Differences of the economic performance of newly founded firms in West- and East Germany. In: Dowling M, Schmude J, Knyphausen-Aufsess D (eds) Advances in Interdisciplinary European Entrepreneurship Research. Lit, Muenster, pp 143-152

Brixy U, Niese M (2004) Analyse von Standorteinflüssen auf das Gründungsgeschehen. In: Fritsch M, Grotz R (eds) Empirische Analysen zum Gründungsgeschehen in Deutschland. Physica, Heidelberg, pp 111–122

Brüderl J, Preisendörfer P, Ziegler R (1992) Survival Chances of Newly Founded Business Organizations. American Sociological Review 57: 227-242

Brüderl J, Schüssler R (1990) Organizational Mortality: The Liabilities of Newness and Adolescence. Administrative Science Quarterly 35: 530-547

Bryk AS, Raudenbush SW (1992) Hierarchical Linear Models. Sage, Newbury Park

Bundesamt für Bauwesen und Raumordnung (2003) Aktuelle Daten zur Entwicklung der Städte, Kreise und Gemeinden. BBR, Bonn

Bundesforschungsanstalt für Landeskunde und Raumordnung (1987) Laufende Raumbeobachtung: Aktuelle Daten zur Entwicklung der Städte, Kreise und Gemeinden 1986. Bonn

Burke A, Görg H, Hanley A (2005) The Survival of New Ventures in Dynamic Versus Static Markets. Discussion Papers on Entrepreneurship, Growth and Public Policy 1205, Max Planck Insitute of Economics, Jena.

Carree MA, Thurik R (2003) The Impact of Entrepreneurship on Economic Growth. In: Acs ZJ, Audretsch DB (eds) Handbook of Entrepreneurship Research. Kluwer, Boston, pp 437-471

Carroll GR, Hannan M (1989) Density Delay in the Evolution of Organizational Populations. Administrative Science Quarterly 34: 411 – 430

Carroll GR, Hannan M (2000) The Demography of Corporations and Industries. Princeton University Press, Princeton (NJ)

Chell E, Haworth J, Brearley S (1991) The Entrepreneurial Personality. Routledge, London

Comanor WS, Wilson TA (1967) Advertising Market Structure and Performance, Review of Economics and Statistics 44: 423-440

Cooke P (2002) Knowledge Economies – Clusters, learning and cooperative advantage. Routledge, London

Cooper A, Dunkelberg WC (1987) Entrepreneurial Research: Old Questions, New Answers and Methodological Issues. American Journal of Small Business 11: 11-23

Cox DR (1972) Regression Models and Life Tables. Journal of the Royal Statistical Society 34: 187–220

Deutsche Bundesbank (German Federal Bank) (various volumes) Monatsberichte (Monthly Reports). Frankfurt a. Main

Doeringer P, Terkla D (1995) Business Strategy and Cross-Industry Clusters, Economic Development Quarterly 9: 225–237

Dunne T, Roberts MJ (1991) Variation in Producer Turnover Across US Manufacturing Industries. In: Geroski PA, Schwalbach J (eds) Entry and Market Contestability: An International Comparison. Basil Blackwell, Oxford, pp 187-203

Evans DS, Jovanovic B (1989) An Estimated Model of Entrepreneurial Choice Under Liquidity Constraints. Journal of Political Economy 97: 808–827

Evans L, Siegfried J (1994) Empirical Studies of Entry and Exit: A Survey of the Evidence. Review of Industrial Organization 9: 121-156

Falck O (2007a) Mayflies and Long-Distance Runners: The Effects of New Business Formation on Industry Growth. Applied Economics Letters 14

Falck O (2007b) Survival Chances of New Businesses: Do Regional Conditions Matter? Applied Economics 39

Falck O, Heblich S (2007) Dynamic Clusters, BGPE Discussion Paper 16

Feldman M (1994a) The Geography of Innovation. Kluwer Academic Publishers, Boston

Feldman M (1994b) Knowledge Complementarily and Innovation. Small Business Economics 6: 363–372

Feldman M, Audretsch DB (1999) Innovation in Cities: Science-Based Diversity, Specialization and Localized Competition. European Economic Review 43: 409–429

Florida R (2002a) Bohemia and Economic Geography. Journal of Economic Geography 2: 55–71

Florida R (2002b) The Rise of the Creative Class. Basic Books, New York

Fotopoulos G, Spence N (1999) Spatial Variation in New Manufacturing Plant Openings: Some Empirical Evidence from Greece. Regional Studies 33: 219-229

Fritsch M (1996) Turbulence and Growth in West Germany: A Comparison of Evidence by Regions and Industries. Review of Industrial Organization 11: 231-251

Fritsch M (2000) Interregional differences in R&D activities – an empirical investigation. European Planning Studies 8: 409-427

Fritsch M (2004) Entrepreneurship, Entry and Performance of New Businesses Compared in two Growth Regimes: East and West Germany. Journal of Evolutionary Economics 14: 525-542

Fritsch M (2007) Introduction: The Effects of New Businesses on Economic Development in the Short, Medium and Long Run. Small Business Economics, Special Issue, in press

Fritsch M, Brixy U (2004) The Establishment File of the German Social Insurance Statistics, Schmollers Jahrbuch / Journal of Applied Social Science Studies 124: 183–190

Fritsch M, Brixy U, Falck O (2006) The Effect of Industry, Region and Time on New Business Survival – A Multi-Dimensional Analysis. Review of Industrial Organization 28, 285-306

Fritsch M, Falck O (2007) New Business Formation by Industry over Space and Time: A Multidimensional Analysis. Regional Studies 41: 157-172

Fritsch M, Grotz R (eds) (2002) Das Gründungsgeschehen in Deutschland - Darstellung und Vergleich der Datenquellen. Physica, Heidelberg

Fritsch M, Mueller P (2004) Effects of New Business Formation on Regional Development Over Time. Regional Studies 38: 961–975

Fritsch M, Mueller P (2006) The Evolution of Regional Entrepreneurship and Growth Regimes. In: Fritsch M, Schmude J (eds) Entrepreneurship in the Region. Springer, New York, pp 225–244

Fritsch M, Mueller P, Weyh A (2005) Direct and Indirect Effects of New Business Formation on Regional Employment. Applied Economics Letters 12: 545–548

Fritsch M, Niese M (2004) Das Ausmaß von Branchen- und Standorteinflüssen auf das regionale Gründungsgeschehen. In: Fritsch M, Grotz R (eds) Empirische Analysen zum Gründungsgeschehen in Deutschland. Physica, Heidelberg, pp 85–110.

Fritsch M, Weyh A (2006) How Large Are the Direct Employment Effects of New Businesses? – An Empirical Investigation. Small Business Economics 27: 245-260

Geroski PA (1995) What Do We Know about Entry? International Journal of Industrial Organization 13: 421–440

Geroski PA, Mata J, Portugal P (2002) Founding Conditions and the Survival of New Firms. Lisboa, Portugal (mimeo)

Glaeser E, Kallal H, Scheinkman J, Schleifer A (1992) Growth of Cities. Journal of Political Economy, 100: 1126–1152

Glaeser E, Kolko J, Saiz A (2001) Consumer City. Journal of Economic Geography 1: 27–50

Goldstein H (1995) Multilevel Statistical Models. Wiley, New York

Gort M, Klepper S (1982) Time Paths in the Diffusion of Product Innovations. Economic Journal 92: 630–653

Grambsch PM, Therneau TM (1994) Proportional Hazards Tests in Diagnostics Based on Weighted Residuals. Biometrika 81: 515–526

Greene WH (2003) Econometric Analysis. Prentice Hall, New York

Greif S (1998) Patentatlas Deutschland – Die Räumliche Struktur der Erfindungstätigkeit. Deutsches Patentamt, Munich

Greif S, Schmiedl D (2002) Patentaltlas Deutschland – Dynamik und Struktur der Erfindertätigkeit. Deutsches Patent- und Markenamt, Munich

Griliches Z (1992) Patent Statistics as Economic Indicator: A Survey. Journal of Economic Literature 28: 1661–1707

Hannan M, Carroll GR (1992) Dynamics of Organizational Populations. Oxford University Press, Oxford

Harhoff D, Stahl K, Woywode M (1998) Legal Form, Growth and Exit of West German Firms. Journal of Industrial Economics 46: 453–488

Holtz-Eakin D, Joulfaian D, Rosen HS (1994) Sticking It Out: Entrepreneurial Survival and Liquidity Constraints. Journal of Political Economy 102: 53–75

Hosmer DW, Lemeshow S (1999) Applied Survival Analysis – Regression Modelling of Time To Event Data. John Wiley & Sons, New York

Huber PJ (1967) The behavior of maximum likelihood estimates under nonstandard conditions, Vol. 1. University of California Press, Berkeley

Hymer S (1976) The International Operations of National Firms. MIT Press, Cambridge, MA

Im KS, Pesaran MH, Shin Y (2002) Testing for Unit Roots in Heterogeneous Panels. DAE Working Papers Amalgamated Series (University of Cambridge) 9526

Jacobs J (1969) The Economy of Cities. Random House, New York

Jaffe A B, Trajtenberg M, Henderson R (1993) Geographic Localization of Knowledge Spillovers as Evidenced by Patent Citations. Quarterly Journal of Economics 63: 577–598

Jenkins SP (2004) Survival Analysis. University of Essex

Johnson P, Parker S (1996) Spatial Variations in the Determinants and Effects of Firm Births and Deaths. Regional Studies 30: 679-688

Johnson PS, Cathcart DG (1979a) The Founders of New Manufacturing Firms: A Note on the Size of their "Incubator" Plants. Journal of Industrial Economics 28: 219-224

Johnson PS, Cathcart DG (1979b) New Manufacturing Firms and Regional Development: Some Evidence from the Northern Region. Regional Studies 13: 269-280

Jovanovic B (2001) Fitness and Age. Journal of Economic Literature 39: 105–119

Keeble D, Walker S, Robson M (1993) New Firm Formation and Small Business Growth: Spatial and Temporal Variations in the United Kingdom, Employment Department, Research Series, No 15, September

Kihlstrom RE, Laffont JJ (1979) A General Equilibrium Theory of Firm Formation Based on Risk Aversion. Journal of Political Economy 87: 719–748

Kim JS (2003) Efficient Estimation for the Proportional Hazards Model with Left-Truncated and "Case 1" Interval-Censored Data. Statistica Sinica 13: 519–537

Klepper S (2001) The Evolution of the U.S. Automobile Industry and Detroit as its Capital. Pittsburgh. Carnegie Mellon University (mimeo)

Klepper S, Simon KL (2000) The Making of an Oligopoly: Firm Survival and Technological Change in the Evolution of the U.S. Tire Industry. Journal of Political Economy 108: 728-760

Klepper S, Sleeper SD (2005) Entry by Spinoffs. Management Science 51: 1291-1306

Krugman P (1991) Geography and Trade. MIT Press, Cambridge, MA.

Lancaster T (1990) The Econometric Analysis of Transition Data. Cambridge University Press, Cambridge

Long JS (1997) Regression Models for Categorical and Limited Dependent Variables. Sage Publications, Thousand Oaks

MacDonald JM (1986) Entry and Exit on the Competitive Fringe. Southern Economic Journal 52: 640-652

Mahmood T (2000) Survival of Newly Founded Businesses: A Log-Logistic Approach. Small Business Economics 14: 223–237

Marshall A (1890) Principles of Economics. Macmillan, London

Marsili O (2002) Technological Regimes and Sources of Entrepreneurship. Small Business Economics 19: 217-215

Mata J, Portugal P (1994) Life Duration of New Firms. Journal of Industrial Economics 42: 227–245

Mata J, Portugal P (2002) The Survival of New Domestic and Foreign Owned Firms. Strategic Management Journal 23: 323–343

Mata J, Portugal P, Guimaraes P (1995) The Survival of New Plants: Start-Up Conditions and Post-Entry Evolution. International Journal of Industrial Organization 35: 607–627

Mayer WJ, Chappell WF (1992) Determinants of Entry and Exit: An Application of the Compounded Bivariate Poisson Distribution to U.S. Industries, 1972-1977. Southern Economic Journal 58: 770-778

Mueller E, Morgan JN (1962) Location Decisions of Manufacturers. American Economic Review 52: 204-217

Mueller P (2006a) Entrepreneurship in the Region: Breeding Ground for Nascent Entrepreneurs? Small Business Economics 27: 41-58

Mueller P (2006b) Exploring the Knowledge Filter: How Entrepreneurship and University-Industry Relations Drive Economic Growth. Research Policy 35: 1499-1508

Nielson GG, Gill RD, Andersen PK, Sorensen TIA (1992): A Counting Process Approach to Maximum Likelihood Estimation in Frailty Models. Scandinavian Journal of Statistics 19: 25–43

Parker S (2005) Economics of Entrepreneurship. Foundations and Trends in Entrepreneurship 1.

Patch, EP (1995) Plant Closings and Employment Loss in Manufacturing. Garland Publishing, New York

Pedroni P (1999) Critical Values for Cointegration Tests in Heterogeneous Panels with Multiple Regressors. Oxford Bulletin of Economics and Statistics, Special Issue: 653–670

Pennings JM (1982) The Urban Quality of Life and Entrepreneurship. Academy of Management Journal 25: 63-79

Persson H (2004) The Survival and Growth of New Establishments in Sweden, 1987–1995. Small Business Economics 23: 423–440

Pfeiffer F, Reize F (2000) Business Start-ups by the Unemployed – An Econometric Analysis Based on Firm Data. Labour Economics 7: 629-63

Piore M, Sabel C (1984) The Second Industrial Divide. Possibilities for Prosperity. Basic Books, New York

Porter M (1990) The Competitive Advantage of Nations. Free Press, New York

Porter M (1998) Clusters and the new economics of competition. Harvard Business Review, November-December: 77-90

Porter M (1998) On Competition. Harvard Business School Press, Boston

Ranger-Moore J (1997) Bigger May be Better, But is Older Wiser? American Sociological Review 62: 903-920

Reynolds PD, Storey DJ, Westhead P (1994) Cross National Comparison of the Variation in New Firm Formation Rates. Regional Studies 27: 443-456

Romer PM (1986) Increasing Returns and Long-Run Growth. Journal of Political Economy 94: 71–102

Rosenbaum DI, Lamort F (1992) Entry, barriers, exit, and sunk costs: an analysis. Applied Economics 24: 297-304

Santarelli E (1998) Start-Up Size and Post-Entry Performance: The Case of Tourism Services in Italy. Applied Economics 30: 157–163

Santerelli E, Vivarelli M (2002) Is Subsidizing Entry an Optimal Policy? Industrial and Corporate Change 11: 39–52

Saxenian A (1994) Regional Advantage: Culture and Competition in Silicon Valley and Rte. 128. Harvard University Press, Cambridge, MA.

Siegel D (1999) Skill-Biased Technological Change: Evidence from a Firm-Level Survey. W.E. Upjohn Institute Press, Kalamazoo, MI.

Snijders TAB, Bosker RJ (1999) Multilevel Analysis: An Introduction to Basic and Advanced Multilevel Modeling. Sage, London

Sorensen O, Audia PG (2000) The Social Structure of Entrepreneurial Activity: Geographic Concentration of Footwear Production in the United States 1940-1989. American Journal of Sociology 106: 224-262

Sorensen O, Stuart TE (2001) Syndication Networks and the Spatial Distribution of Venture Capital Investments. American Journal of Sociology 106: 1546-1588

Statistisches Bundesamt (Federal Statistical Office) (various volumes) Fachserie 18, Volkswirtschaftliche Gesamtrechnung (National Accounting). Metzler-Poeschel, Stuttgart

Steil F (1999) Determinanten regionaler Unterschiede in der Gründungsdynamik, eine empirische Analyse für die neuen Bundesländer. ZEW Wirtschaftsanalysen 34. Nomos, Baden-Baden

Sterlacchini A (1994) The Birth of New Firms in Italian Manufacturing. Journal of Industry Studies 1: 77-90

Storey DJ (1994) Understanding the Small Business Sector. Routledge, London

Storey DJ (2003) Entrepreneurship, Small and Medium Sized Enterprises and Public Policies. In Acs Z, Audretsch DB (eds) Handbook of Entrepreneurship Research, Kluwer, Boston, pp 473–511.

Suárez FF, Utterback JM (1995) Dominant Design and the Survival of Firms. Strategic Management Journal 16: 415-430

Sutaria V (2001) The Dynamics of New Firm Formation. Ashgate, Aldershot

Sutaria V, Hicks D (2004) New firm formation: Dynamics and determinants. Annals of Regional Science 38: 241-262

Sutton J (1997) Gibrat's Legacy. Journal of Economic Literature 35: 40–59

Tveterås R, Eide GE (2000) Survival of New Plants in Different Industry Environment in Norwegian Manufacturing: A Semi-Proportional Cox Model Approach. Small Business Economics 14: 65-82

Van Stel A, Storey D (2004) The Link Between Firm Births and Job Creation: Is there a Upas Tree Effect? Regional Studies 38: 893-909

Von Hippel E (1994) Sticky Information and the Locus of Problem Solving: Implications for Innovation. Management Science 40: 429–439

Wagner J (1994) The Post-Entry Performance of New Small Firms in German Manufacturing Industries. Journal of Industrial Economics 42: 141-154

Wagner J (2004) Are Young and Small Firms Hothouses for Nascent Entrepreneurs? Applied Economics Quarterly 50: 379–391

Wagner J, Sternberg R (2004) Start-up activities, individual characteristics, and the regional milieu: Lessons for entrepreneurship support policies from German micro data. Annals of Regional Science 38: 219-240

White H (1980) A heteroscedasticity-consistent covariance matrix estimator and a direct test for heteroskedasticity. Econometrica 48: 817-830

Williams RL (2000) A note on robust variance estimation for cluster-correlated data. Biometrics 56: 645–646

Winter SG (1984) Schumpeterian Competition in Alternative Technological Regimes. Journal of Economic Behavior and Organization 5: 287-320

Womack J, Jones D, Roos D (1990) The Machine that Changed the World: The Story of Lean Production. Rawson and Associates, New York

# Index

Printing: Krips bv, Meppel
Binding: Stürtz, Würzburg